NORTH BEND BETWEEN

THE WORLD WARS: 1919-1941

BY

DICK & JUDY WAGNER

Dick Wagner

Judy Wagner

Cover panorama of Coos Bay Bridge courtesy Coos Historical and Maritime Museum.

DEDICATION

To Pat Choat Pierce, community activist in the finest North Bend tradition.

Library of Congress Control Number: 2005908495
ISBN: 0-937861-67-7

Printed in U. S. A. by Wegferd Publications.

Published by: Bygones
                       P. O. Box 1558
                       North Bend, OR 97459

Bookstores, libraries or individuals please contact Bygones for information
regarding acquiring copies of this work.

TABLE OF CONTENTS

North Bend looking north, many buildings constructed in the 1920s and 1930s. Late 1940s photo.   Courtesy Clair Jones.

PREFACE

North Bend experienced two event filled decades between World Wars I and II. Many of the city's substantial commercial buildings in use today date from 1919-1941. During this period a number of significant public projects were undertaken and several prominent citizens built homes.

Fire was a constant threat to the city's wooden structures. North Bend's neighbor city, Marshfield (now Coos Bay), had a serious blaze in 1922 that destroyed Front Street. North Bend's City Council in August 1923 enacted a downtown building code that required "fire proof" construction. Concrete became the building material of choice.

We have tried to treat the principal buildings, specifically those designed by well-known Portland architect John E. Tourtellotte, (the Hotel North Bend, I.O.O.F. building, Liberty Theater, Cutlip building, and Roosevelt School), but have not attempted to cover all construction of the era.

Although we have dedicated this volume to the years between 1919 and 1941, we recognize that history is not tidy. To provide useful background we have reviewed earlier events and have occasionally added contemporary details.

Our format begins with two former industrial sites, Mountain States Power and Kruse and Banks Shipyard, along the bayfront at the south end of the city. We proceed north through downtown to the McCullough Bridge. The second Shoreacres home is not within the boundaries of the city but its owner Louis J. Simpson, founder of the City of North Bend, continued to play an active role in community life even though no longer a resident. We have also included a few topics of general interest not tied to a specific building. Locations are identified on the map pages 36-37.

While perusing the following pages, the reader might find it useful to refer to *Louie Simpson's North Bend* (1986 or 2002 printing). Several articles make reference to buildings and/or events detailed in that prior work.

In addition to the volume noted above readers might also find *L. J.: The Uncommon Life of Louis Jerome Simpson* (Bygones, 2003) of interest.

We are captivated by our city's past, enjoy the time spent delving into it and, hopefully, bringing it alive for others. We collaborated on both the research and the writing so the discerning reader will notice our differing styles.

ACKNOWLEDGMENTS

We are indebted to many individuals who shared family information, recollections and photos. They helped make what we have written more complete and accurate. Thank you to the staffs at the North Bend and Coos Bay Libraries. Special appreciation to Vicki Wiese, Curator of the Coos Historical and Maritime Museum, for help in finding and using museum images. Again we were pleased to work with Edi and Karen Wegfahrt of Wegferd Publications. We especially thank Pat Choat Pierce for her editorial wisdom.

INTRODUCTION

The pulse of the new City of North Bend, born 1903, quickened then slowed. Four remarkable boom years were followed by five years of stagnation. The slowdown was largely the result of the national Panic of 1907. Furthermore, the area was resource dependent and its well being hinged on the fluctuating demand for and price of timber and its products. The economic swings between affluence and adversity continued into the decade that brought the country into World War I.

Louis J. Simpson, founder and the city's first mayor, resigned in May 1915. The January 1915 death of his father, Asa Meade Simpson, required L. J. Simpson's attention to family businesses headquartered in San Francisco. Also, he and wife Cassie moved from the city to live year round at Shoreacres, their ocean side home. Within a year of the elder Simpson's death, the Simpson Lumber Company's Porter Mill, timberlands and other North Bend holdings were sold to Philip Buehner and Son. Other Simpson property, particularly real estate, was retained by the family controlled Simpson Estate Company.

The August 1916 completion of the rail link between the bay area and Eugene was a notable event of this period. The well-celebrated occasion marked the area's integration with Oregon and its decreasing orientation to San Francisco. Rail service was, however, a late comer to our coast. By 1916 the use of autos had expanded, organized groups lobbied for more and better roads and bay residents saw their first airplanes.

The United States' 1917 entry into the World War gave the region a temporary boost with full employment. The U. S. Emergency Shipping Board, for exam-

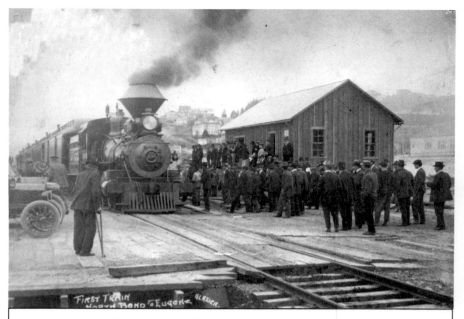

First North Bend to Eugene train.
Courtesy Coos Historical and Maritime Museum.

ple, contracted with Kruse and Banks' shipyard to build a number of large wooden vessels for its fleet. The yard's workforce more than doubled to over 480 men becoming one of the county's largest. War's end in November 1918 brought retrenchment. In 1919 the shipyard had cut back to 150 workers.

The peacetime readjustment period was also the time of a worldwide influenza epidemic. During 1918 to 1920 numbers of area residents succumbed to the flu or its deadly complication, pneumonia. (Influenza returned in 1927 and again caused serious problems on the bay). Settlement of the L. D. Kinney land claims clearing expansion to the south and the Simpson Estate Company's sale of some northern lots to William R. Robertson (Robertson Land Company) for the creation

Martha Buehner hits the railroad bridge, 1924.

of Simpson Heights were milestones in the city's growth.

By 1920 North Bend entered a new period of downtown construction and business vitality. In 1922-23 all business fronts were occupied. Principal "fire proof" concrete construction included the Hotel North Bend, I.O.O.F. building, Liberty Theater, American Legion Hall, Cutlip building, and Roosevelt School.

Early in 1924 all city streets were signed and houses numbered in preparation for the free home postal delivery service scheduled for October.

Peter Loggie, Henry Kern, Fred Hollister, Fred Magnusson, Dr. Philip Keizer, John Greves, Robert Banks, M. Sayle Taylor and Lyle Chappell were some who played leading roles in civic life during the 1920s. Their work with the city council, North Bend Chamber of Commerce, hospital, schools and fraternal groups

helped North Bend mature.

Others, as well as those mentioned above, made their contributions. James A. Allen, for example, an early North Bend businessman, ran the North Bend Shingle Mill, organized in 1904 with L. J. Simpson, and was the first owner of the North Bend Newsstand on Sherman, just south of the Castle/Winsor Building. In late 1918 he ordered construction of the Allen Apartments, 2334-52 Sherman Avenue. Concrete bulkheading, done in early 1921, permitted five garages in the bank below the apartments.

In 1920, although Mr. Allen moved to Florence, Oregon, his business interests continued here with a partnership, the Allen & Curl grocery, located in the Odd Fellows Building. In May 1924 this became Allen & Company with Allen buying out H. J. Curl and joined by T. T. Kohout. The business lasted only until September when a chain, Twentieth Century Grocers, bought them out.

James Allen was one of a sizeable North Bend group who opposed Oregon prohibition. Prohibition came to Oregon in 1915. Selling liquor was illegal but personal possession was not. The law was widely flouted in Coos County. The day before Oregon law took effect, Edgar McDaniel, editor, *Coos Bay Harbor* (North Bend's weekly newspaper), made the rounds of the saloons collecting his printing bills. Booze sold at half price so McDaniel took wagon loads of "in kind" payment back to the large basement under his printing office. Years later, whenever the "Do It While Living Club" gathered for cards and conversation in the printing office back room, McDaniel furnished the liquid refreshment. The McDaniel family, like many others in town, made their own home brewed beer. They produced five gallons a week, bottled by the quart - bottle caps the most costly part of the process.

National prohibition, 1920-33, reinforced the demand for forbidden products delivered by boat from Canada or by car or truck from private South Slough stills. Bellhops at the Hotel North Bend knew where to find liquor for hotel guests and furnished information on the local bordellos as well. "The Sheridan Rooms," 1840 Sheridan, were especially notorious. Certain float houses, tied to the Montana street bridge and at the foot of Washington Avenue, were also suspect.

Garages and gas stations, fueling the spread of the auto, commanded more and more storefront locations in the 1920s, 1930s and into the 1940s - Gurnea's, on the north east corner of Sherman and Washington, Sunrise, on the north west corner of Sheridan and Washington. Later, the north west corner of Sherman and Washington, now a city parking lot, hosted a Mobil station. Gilmore Gas, first located at Union and Virginia in 1935, moved to 1900 Sherman Avenue. Their radio advertising broadcast this memorable jingle:

Blue Green gas
Blue Green gas
Pour it on your belly
Rub it on your ass
There's no one on the highway
You can't pass
Unless they're using Blue Green gas.

The most infamous personality to appear locally was Ku Klux Klan lecturer, C. R. Mathis. He spoke at Eckhoff Hall in early August 1924, touting his organization's legitimacy with the claim that sixty-two percent of all Protestant ministers were members. His message endorsed white supremacy and declared opposition to Catholics, Jews, bootleggers and lawbreakers of all kinds.

North Bend's good times ended with the February 1926 fire that destroyed Stout Mill A (formerly the Porter Mill). Immediately, several hundred men were out of work and the economic consequences rippled through the community. In July, the Stout Company also closed Mill B, a result of the lumber market decline. A local recession was underway, one that would deepen and lengthen with the 1929 stock market crash and the national depression of the 1930s.

The Great Depression seriously affected everyday commerce. The First National Bank of North Bend closed, in order to prevent failure, well before the national "bank holiday." It held many mortgages and

Gilmore Gas Station, Sherman at California, late 1930s.
Courtesy Coos Historical and Maritime Museum.

Mill B, circa 1940s, located south of where Vermont Avenue would come through to the bay.

They would accept it and use it. The City of North Bend stood behind the issue and today would redeem any pieces returned to it.

Local script though useful did not prevent the crippling losses caused by the depression. The newspapers of the 1930s were filled with lists of property that Coos County seized from owners whose taxes were too far in arrears. Indeed the county made 1933 property tax free in order to lessen the burden on the public. Worse, as unemployment grew, so did crime such as theft. At its own worst time, North Bend let the streetlights go dark because the city could not afford electricity. Yet, even in the gloomiest years, there was an occasional flicker of hope, like the pilchard fishing boom in the mid-1930s.

The May 1937 death of businessman Henry Buehner, perhaps tied to depression reverses, was one of the local tragedies. Buehner had been fishing with Fred Magnusson, architect, and A. Purdy, Portland mechanical engineer. They were returning from Gold Beach when Buehner complained of being ill and had the car stopped. He stepped some distance from the auto, took a pistol from his fishing creel, put the gun in his mouth and fired. No motive was given for Buehner's action though Magnusson reported his friend seemed depressed.

Recovery from the depression came in fits and starts. Public

other loans on which payments were not being made. With the bank closed, and many people hoarding money, including gold and silver coin, local businessmen had the city council do what other communities across the land were doing – issue emergency money.

Depression script, like North Bend's 1933 "myrtlewood money" (denominations printed on circular blanks of myrtlewood), were used in communities as ready cash. While beyond the Constitution (only Congress can authorize money), the need was such that no one cared about technicalities. The *Harbor* in March 1932 had run notice that Tenino, Washington, was using wooden money. That probably inspired Mayor Edgar McDaniel to champion the idea. Local businesses ran ads declaring that "myrtlewood money is good money."

Samples of "myrtlewood money" issued in 1933.

works, offering employment and a flow of money to communities where there were funded projects, helped restore more normal commercial life. Along the Oregon coast, five major bridges were built, the largest and most impressive the bridge over Coos Bay completed in 1936. This bridge permitted retirement of the ferries used to connect the Roosevelt Highway (Highway 101) between North Bend and Glasgow. North Bend City Hall also benefited from federal public works funds. Yet another project, an outgrowth of the 1930s, was the airport at North Bend. In 1942 the Navy took over the facility for wartime use and made many improvements before returning it to the city post war.

During the 1919-1941 period North Bend prospered, faltered and with federal assistance recovered. Her citizens rebuilt her commercial center and kept faith with the city despite numerous setbacks. The next generation preserved the city's existence and participated in great prosperity and growth. But that story is for others to tell.

Power station, looking east.　　　Courtesy City of North Bend.

Completing an approach road to the bridge over Coos Bay.

1. MOUNTAIN STATES POWER
Bay front, between State and Lombard Streets

North Bend's electrical utility changed its name from Oregon Power Company to Mountain States Power in 1918. More than a name change was needed. The plant, located on the bay front near the former Simpson Porter Mill, never had adequate capacity to handle the area's growth.

In July 1923 the power company projected that by September 1 "interruptions will be few and far between." The company asked its customers for "due consideration of our difficulties and of our efforts to provide a better service." Unfortunately for users, service did not improve. The North Bend Chamber of Commerce, given to boosting not knocking, criticized the power company in late September 1923 for the off and on again supply over a ten day period, that seriously affected the mills, hospital, movies, every business and home. Undoubtedly heavy personal and other pressures were brought to bear on A. L. Martin, the local manager.

Potential profit, as well as mounting customer complaints, motivated Mountain States Power Company to announce, in December 1923, a new $600,000 to $750,000 North Bend power plant. About 900 new service connections throughout the county and a 2500 horsepower demand drove the expansion. Property was purchased from The Stout Lumber Company, owners of the old Porter mill.

Construction began in 1924. Manager Martin noted that the new facility's power was being integrated with that of the C. A. Smith mill in Marshfield so that if one source failed the other could carry the load. (When the *Coos Bay Times*, predecessor to *The World*, reported this news in November the paper did not mention that the plant was in North Bend. North Bend's *Coos Bay Harbor* commenting on the omission editorialized "Nobody really cared because the

Times twisted the facts, for all here realize that the paper is against North Bend first, last and all the time.")

May 1, 1925, Mayor Phil Keizer dedicated the $730,000 Mountain States plant and turned the master wheel that started the steam turbine. The Butterfly Gardens orchestra played while guests enjoyed ice cream, punch and wafers. Martin gave cigars to the men and carnations to the women.

The new plant drew water from the bay and used hog fuel (sawdust and wood scraps) to generate steam for its turbines. Barges brought fuel economically to the

Power station with barges of hog fuel at left. Kruse and Banks Shipyard at right. Photo looking west circa 1943. Courtesy Coos Historical and Maritime Museum.

site. As sawmills unpredictably shutdown interrupting the supply of hog fuel, Mountain States installed a backup fuel oil system. The plant expected to generate 5,000 kilowatts of power and meet growth demands for several years.

Unfortunately power generation was a dirty business. Everything in the smokestack's wind path was covered in soot. The emissions were unhealthy and made household chores such as cleaning and laundry more burdensome.

Mountain States expanded again in 1929. The company bought the North Bend ballpark on the bay front and other adjacent land. Byllesby Engineering and Management designed the project. They added 50' in width, 165' in length and 70' in height to the existing plant. Three 185' high steel stacks were built to discharge furnace gases. Capacity increased to 10,000 kilowatts. The *Harbor*, August 1, 1930, detailed some of the engineering feats.

The area received more power and along with it increased amounts of ash and soot that drifted citywide. Citizens' love/hate relationship with the power company continued.

Hydroelectric power eventually replaced locally generated sources. Pacific Power replaced Mountain States. Little but power lines and poles remain of what once was a key element of the community's infrastructure.

2. KRUSE AND BANKS SHIPBUILDING CORPORATION

A drastic reduction in the needed work force and a devastating fire characterized many years for the Kruse and Banks Shipyard between the two World Wars.

Located on the bay front between Lewis and Highway Streets, the firm reached its peak development during World War I when it expanded from three to five shipways and employed nearly 500 workers. The expansion was driven by contracts to supply Hough and Ferris type hulls for the U. S. Shipping Board's emergency fleet. These merchant ships replaced tonnage lost

Kruse and Banks Shipyard, circa 1919, looking east. Courtesy Coos Historical and Maritime Museum.

to German submarines. Kruse and Banks was, for a time, one of the county's largest employers. The company even had its own band that played for launchings and special occasions.

After the war, employment at the yard declined. For example, in May 1925 there were 85 men at work. However this was a prosperous time for the area and construction was booming. The company helped fill a need by doing framing for house builders, supplying sash and doors, and doing specialty built-in work.

July 30, 1933, a fire originating from the nearby Western Battery and Separator Company quickly swept through the shipyard. Only the office building, planer shed, machine shop and wharf, all at the north end, were saved. Essential rebuilding soon began.

During their notable history the firm built a variety of vessels including steam and gas schooners, tugs, barges, scows, the ferry *Roosevelt* and the last two tall ships of the Coos Bay, the five masted *K. V. Kruse* (1919) and the four masted *North Bend* (1920).

To recount the extraordinary contributions of the Kruse and Banks Shipyard to the war efforts during the 1940s would take a book in itself. As we said earlier in the introduction, "...that story is for others to tell." We'll only mention that the shipyard was a veritable hub of activity producing wooden ships capable of many functions, like minesweeping, that metal-laden vessels could not do.

The Kruse and Banks story began in 1903 when the era of Simpson shipbuilding ended. K. V. Kruse, a master builder for Simpson, went out on his own, first leasing a site on the bay about a mile north of Marshfield. He was joined in 1905 by Robert Banks, friend and fellow worker at the Dickie Brothers' San Francisco

shipyard in the 1890s. Kruse was the principal designer and builder, Banks became the business manager.

The partnership moved their operations to the former Simpson shipyard near the Porter Mill (North Bend) in 1907. The company remained at their bay front location until the business closed its books in 1946 having sold their property to Weyerhaeuser in 1945.

Following the death of K. V. Kruse in 1936 at age eighty-two, Fred Kruse assumed his father's position in the company. Robert Banks remained very active in real estate development and community concerns long after the shipyard closure. He worked as a marine surveyor until the last few years before his death in 1964, at age ninety-four.

Four masted schooner *North Bend*, built 1920, by Kruse and Banks. The last tall ship built on the Coos Bay. A tug smokestack visible. Courtesy Coos Historical and Maritime Museum.

3. RYAN'S GROCERY & MEAT MARKET
2506 Sherman Avenue

This commercial building arose amidst controversy. In early 1924, when residents of the Sherman Hill area learned that G. W. Shelley planned to build a store on the southwest corner of Sherman and Maryland, they organized resistance. In March, forty people from the vicinity petitioned Shelley to change his plans in consideration of his neighbors and friends. Their argument was that a business operation was unsuitable for their residential area and was detrimental to nearby property values, for example the lovely Buehner (formerly Winsor) house, on the north west corner of the intersection.

Business interests won out. John F. Ryan, who relocated from Aberdeen, Washington, opened his bungalow style grocery store May 1, 1924. In February 1929 Ryan moved his grocery from the bungalow location to 1937 Sherman.

By 1933 Ryan's original store was Warren's Bungalow Grocery. The building survives as the Bungalow Grocery.

After his rocky introduction to the community, Ryan became a strong advocate for North Bend. He was one of the organizers of the highway bridge celebration in 1936. In 1937, responding to the need for housing, Mr. & Mrs. Ryan engaged Sig Anderson to build six apartments on the southwest corner of Sherman and Delaware, all in a two-story building with attic. Ryan served as North Bend mayor January 1941 to March 1944.

Bungalow Grocery in 2005.

4. ROOSEVELT SCHOOL
2389 Sherman Avenue

School lunch token circa 1940s. 1 inch diameter.

Early in the city's history, L. J. and Cassie Simpson set aside sixteen lots in block 66 atop Sherman hill as the prospective site for a new "in town" residence. The building of their Shoreacres home and Cassie's death in 1921 left the future of the lots in limbo. The situation changed, however, in February 1923 when L. J. Simpson, recently remarried, put these lots up for sale. There were no buyers at the prices and conditions set. The property was sold to a long time business acquaintance, Henry G. Kern who, owner of the local iron works, was a county commissioner and a school board member.

Around this time the school board, in response to public pressure, was looking for another school site. Citizens voted a $50,000 bond in December 1923, but there was no public consensus regarding either the Central School site or "Simpson hill." In January 1924 the board voted 3 to 1 (Kern abstaining) to purchase the ex-Simpson site from Kern for $5,500 plus 1923 taxes and any street assessments.

Prior to the vote, members of the school board visited these and other sites and publicly concluded the Kern owned property was the best alternative.

The board's most vocal opponent was Mrs. Herbert Armstrong, wife of Menasha's chief, who in letters to the North Bend newspaper accused the board of ignoring the will of the people and behaving like "Tammany Hall." She claimed that people were taxed to build the schools and then the board did what it pleased with the money. Her reasoned arguments and a petition drive not withstanding, the board's decision held.

By February 1924, the board hired noted Portland architect J. E. Tourtellotte to draw the plans and supervise construction. First sketches provided for a two story concrete building finished in stucco. Plans detailed eleven classrooms, teachers' lounge, cafeteria, principal's office and probably a lunchroom. The design permitted additions as necessary.

In April, Hoover & McNeil, builders of the new Liberty Theater, were awarded a $32,000 construction contract. Heating ($3250) went to W. S. Fleming; plumbing ($2270) to Schroeder & Hildebrand, and electrical ($222) to E. J. Arms. Contract terms required the building to be ready for use by September 15, 1924.

The building was ready for the opening of school September 8. The first year Roosevelt School (named for President Theodore Roosevelt) took all sixth through eighth grade students, except sixth graders who lived in Bangor. In 1925 it became the junior high taking seventh and eighth graders. In 1926 fifth and sixth graders were added.

Roosevelt School was last used by the school district in spring, 2000. The Celebration Center now owns the building and has located there.

Roosevelt School. Courtesy
Coos Historical and Maritime Museum.

5. PRESBYTERIAN COMMUNITY CHURCH

2100 Union Ave.

In early 1923 members of the Presbyterian Church decided on a new building. They had outgrown their wooden structure, built 1903-04, one lot south of the south west corner of Union on Montana. Building committee members – all leading citizens - were Peter Loggie, chair, Henry Buehner, John Greves, J. A. Wilkinson, Cecil Brown, C. A. Smith, Mrs. George Hazer, Mrs. Fred Hollister, Mrs. Wm. Vaughan and Mrs. Russell Keizer.

Fred Magnusson, prominent local architect, drew the plans for a bungalow style building and craftsman

Photo courtesy Coos Historical and Maritime Museum.

interior. His drawings were displayed in a window of the Chamber of Commerce and contributions welcomed.

In January 1924 Hagquist & Bjorquist contracted to build the church on three lots at the south west corner of Union and Washington. The building was meant as a community meeting place as well as for worship. The main floor seated 400. Additionally, 250 persons could be accommodated in the social room, connected by folding doors. There were eight Sunday school rooms. A church parlor had wicker chairs and a large fireplace. A basement dining room, with a fully equipped kitchen, sat 250. Oregon fir, with a clear varnish, was used throughout the interior of the building.

The church cornerstone, visible today, was laid in March 1924. Speakers included L. J. Simpson and Sen. Charles Hall. A construction error placed the steps, porch and part of the porch columns beyond the church's property line. Church officials appeared before city council to apologize for the error. The result, a narrowed Union Avenue, remains.

The new stucco finished church cost $25,000 and was dedicated Sunday, June 29, 1924. Under Dr. J. E. Snyder, who came to the church in 1922, membership grew to 150 in 1924. The mortgage was paid in 1930.

Barbara Jean Simpson, L. J. Simpson's daughter, married Thomas Griffin here in 1948.

The Presbyterians left for another new building and location in 1967. Subsequently, the old church stood periodically vacant. In the 1990s a partnership refurbished the site. The building was rewired, replumbed, a new roof added and pews were taken apart and the wood used to repair interior damage.

Unity by the Bay has owned and occupied the property since 2000.

6. AMERICAN LEGION BUILDING

2090 Union Avenue

In the early 1920s men of the local American Legion Sunset Post 34 wanted North Bend to have a modern dance pavilion. The Legion leased meeting space in the basement of the First National Bank building (Brick Block).

By February 1922 they took an option on Charles S. Kaiser's property on the north west corner of Union and Washington as well as an adjoining lot owned by Fred Hollister and John Greves. Purchase of these lots cost $2800 plus street and sewer assessments. The Legion planned to finance construction through sale of stock in the building.

Portland architect, John E. Tourtellotte, was to draw up plans for a large concrete dance hall building with cloak, checking and rest rooms plus a confectionery stand. However, at a late March 1922 meeting, Legion members voted to accept plans submitted by local architect, Fred Magnusson. The group organized as the Legion Building Corporation with a capitalization of $25,000 and in cooperation with a committee of the North Bend Chamber of Commerce launched a final subscription drive.

During March workers used fifty sticks of dynamite to clear the land. In April, G. A. Perkins and Son excavated for the basement. By May 1 Hedges and Huls, builders of the Hotel North Bend, obtained the general construction contract at $17,760. Huls was in charge of the job. Total cost ran a bit over $21,000.

The building was completed in thirty days and turned over to the Legion at noon on Monday, July 3, 1922. The Tower Orchestra played for the opening

dance that began Monday afternoon, ran late into the evening and resumed again Tuesday afternoon continuing long into Tuesday night. A winter dancing season began in October on Wednesday and Saturday nights.

The dance floor was 80' x 100' and built to three thicknesses. The surface was dressed with three-eight's inch hardwood to give the desired resiliency. In 1924 boxing matches were held there.

September 1926 the Legion leased the hall to M. A. Gallow of Eugene, operator of the Winter Gardens. Business slowed after Stout Mill A's fire in February. During the early 1930s the Trianon Dance Hall/Ballroom occupied the property. Jack Routledge was the manager in 1933.

January 29 through February 1, 1930, the Post put on an indoor circus with assembled acts, a number of them from the Al G. Barnes organization. Milton Taylor, head clown with Barnes, was wintering in the bay

American Legion Hall in 1922. Sign on left advertises a dance. Courtesy Coos Historical and Maritime Museum.

area with his mother. Taylor's wife was a well-known rider with the Barnes circus.

In September 1934 Carl Golder, of Golder's Auto Parts, bought the building from Pacific Savings and Loan of Tacoma, paying cash. (The mortgage probably was foreclosed during the depression.) Golder's business occupied the building until the early 21st century. The Golder family continues to own the property.

7. LIBERTY THEATER

Sherman Avenue at Washington

The Joy Theater, 2036 Sherman, like many others across the nation during World War I, changed its name to Liberty Theater in March 1918. Its new electric light bulb sign flashed "Liberty." Manager Dennis Hull, in the August 3, 1923, *Coos Bay Harbor*, announced plans for a new building at a new location, the south

Artist sketch of Liberty Theater, in *Coos Bay Harbor*, August 24, 1923. Courtesy North Bend Public Library.

Liberty Theater sign at its original location. 1919 photo. Courtesy Coos Historical and Maritime Museum.

west corner of Washington and Sherman Avenues.

A theater was not what Robert Banks, of Kruse and Banks shipbuilding, had in mind for his lot. Banks, after purchasing the land from an estate in 1919, told the *Harbor* that plans for a two-story, concrete, modern garage building estimated to cost $16,000, were on hold. The *Harbor* estimated, from deed tax stamps, that Banks had paid about $2100 for the lot. (The lot had cost $100 in 1903 and was valued at $8000 during the speculative boom ending in 1907).

There was no further public development until August 24, 1923, when the *Harbor* ran a front-page sketch of a theater that Robert Banks proposed for construction. Portland architect J. E. Tourtellotte designed the building in a Spanish "baronial" style, suggesting a mystical and romantic appearance. A pipe organ was promised.

The building's overall cost was estimated at about $75,000. Hoover & McNeil, of Albany, won the construction contract. Plumbing was done by A. J. Eberhardt of North Bend, while J. A. Drake of Albany did the electrical work. Furnishings and decorating came from B. F. Shearer of Seattle. The theater's concrete exterior was bleached white.

The building was 50' wide, 100' long and 50' high. The interior was 48' by 75' with a stage measuring 20' x 27'. Seating capacity was 750 counting the main floor, mezzanine and small balcony. Most seats were overstuffed with spring cushions. The fifty-four loge seats were upholstered in velour. The 9' x 20' projection room high in the front of the theater had two, latest model, Simplex machines that projected an image ninety feet to the gold fiber Gardiner screen. Leonard Ingeman was projectionist for the Liberty. The Coos Bay Amusement Co., formed by Dennis Hull, Robert Marsden, Jr. and John C. Noble, operated the house.

The interior painted murals told the story of a Spanish prince on a search for a princess. He rode a snow-white charger as he left his castle. The opposite wall had the princess consulting a witch about the coming of the prince. The theater's Wurlitzer organ was the second largest in Oregon, exceeded only by one at the Liberty Theater in Portland. Rex Stratton played the Wurlitzer.

The Liberty Theater opened on Easter Sunday April 20, 1924, quite appropriate for the reborn Liberty Theater. Among the four groups of music Stratton played was von Suppe's "Poet and Peasant" overture. (In November 1925 Stratton resigned his position to become the organist at the new Egyptian Theater in Marshfield.) The world premier showing of "The Fight-

ing Coward," starring Ernest Torrence, Noah Beery and Mary Astor, among others, headlined the program. The film was adapted from Booth Tarkington's novel "Magnolia." Hal Roach's Rascals also entertained in the film "Big Business." Prices for the opening show were 25c children, 50c adults, and 75c loges.

Moving pictures shown during 1925 included Eric Von Stroheim's "Greed," and Douglas Fairbanks in "Robin Hood." In 1926 Charlie Chaplin's "The Gold Rush" and Lon Chaney in "The Phantom of the Opera" came to town. Then, in the late 1920s, the movie industry changed dramatically as "talkies" became the rage.

In mid-May, 1929, Dennis Hull announced that the Liberty would soon follow the Egyptian Theater, installing Western Electric equipment and showing Vitaphone talking pictures. July 9, 10 and 11, 1929, the sound era opened in North Bend with "Speakeasy," a

New Liberty Theater with old sign, late 1920s.
Courtesy Coos Historical and Maritime Museum.

Fox Movietone feature starring Paul Page and Lola Lane. Patrons were promised they would hear the sounds of New York City, from subways and Grand Central Station to Madison Square Garden and Belmont racetrack.

"All Quiet on the Western Front" was shown to capacity houses for four nights in July 1930. February 1931 a new neon sign was installed, replacing the flashing electric light bulb sign. The theater sign was likely all that had been transferred from the old to the new building.

The depression forced the Liberty to close for the greater part of the summer, into fall, 1932. In November, Hull announced that the Liberty would reopen November 9 with the football film, "All American" starring Richard Arlen. Prices were reduced to 25c adults, 10c children.

When the Port Theater opened in 1953, the Liberty became a "second run" venue. In June 1959, the Little Theater on the Bay group (LTOB) produced "The Tender Trap" in the Liberty Theater, their first production in a building they now own.

8. CUTLIP'S ICE CREAM PLANT
Sheridan Avenue at Washington

In early 1923, Largo A. Cutlip, of Aberdeen, Washington, leased the former Coos Bay Fish & Canning Co. ice plant that had been vacant for a year. His goal was to operate an ice cream factory for the wholesale market.

When production began in April 1923, the first day's output was 200 gallons of ice cream, doubling to 400 gallons the second day. The plant made a variety of frozen products from sherbet to Neapolitan brick. The plant's first shipments went to North Bend, Lakeside, Allegany, Sumner, Empire and Marshfield.

The summer of 1923 proved extremely busy with sales from areas outside North Bend and Marshfield equaling those from the two towns. His customer service area was a fifty miles radius from the plant. In preparation for summer 1924, Cutlip purchased a new $3,000 ice machine and other equipment.

1924's business proved so good that in July Cutlip announced plans for a new plant at the south east corner of Sheridan and Washington, on land purchased from Charles S. Winsor. Cutlip estimated that property, building and equipment would cost about $25,000. Cutlip engaged J. E. Tourtellotte, Portland, as his architect and on August 15, 1924, the *Coos Bay Harbor* ran a sketch of the proposed design.

The general contract to build the 40' x 60' con-

Liberty Theater with the neon sign acquired in 1931.

crete building went to Hoover & McNeil, Albany, who did the Liberty Theater and Roosevelt School. Construction bids awarded, as reported by the *Harbor* on August 22, 1924, included E. J. Arms electrical and A. J. Eberhardt plumbing. The general contractors were to have the building up in sixty days. Final cost figures proved just over $30,000.

The two-story building, with living quarters for the Cutlip family on the second floor, had steam heat throughout. A crystal ice plant that froze water, vats for curing cream and a $1,000 rotary churn were among the new equipment purchased. Manufactured butter was added to the firm's dairy line. The plant opened in November 1924, offering such ice cream flavors as Golden Poppy, Hawaiian Delight and Tutti Fruitti.

Again, in October 1925 the firm sought bids on a 30' x 50' annex to fill the space between the new Cutlip building and the Coos Hotel. In 1929 storage space was once more increased.

Ice cream in a sealed paper cup and eaten with a paper spoon was a treat Cutlip's introduced to the area in 1927. It sold for a nickel. In 1930 the firm acquired an Eskimo Pie machine; Cutlip's product sold as "Zero Bars." In 1934, with prohibition ended, Cutlip used his large storage capacity to become a wholesaler for five brands of beer.

In 1936 when fire threatened L. J. Simpson's Shoreacres home, L. A. Cutlip provided several trucks so that the Simpsons could pack their belongings and transport them to safety.

Cutlip's ice cream business endured until 1979, always a wholesale firm.

L. A. Cutlip served as North Bend mayor from 1935 to 1941.

Cutlip's Ice Cream plant after 1934. The words above the arch where the auto is entering read "L. A. Cutlip Wholesale Liquor Dealer." Courtesy Coos Historical and Maritime Museum.

9. DEAN BUILDING

2097 Sherman Avenue

Late in 1921 G. Whittley sold a lot on the north east corner of Sherman and Washington to C. R. Dean, E. E. Dean, et al., for $7000. (In 1919 Gorst & King had wanted the lot but it was not available.) The new owners built a large two-story concrete garage that, when finished in May 1922, was leased for some years to the Gurnea Service Station. Gurnea relocated from 2042 Sherman and carried a full line of tires and accessories.

Heavy timbers were used in construction. The building was sided with metal lath, had a fire resistant roof and the exterior finished in stucco. There was a full basement. The floor, level with Sherman Avenue, had an entrance and corner service. There was a rest room for ladies and gentlemen and a display room with large plate glass window. The floor below, to the east, housed the machine shop and storage.

In the 1930s Sunrise Service Station occupied the site. (Sunrise had organized in 1924, building a two story garage at the corner of Sheridan and Washington.) In the early 1980s a carpet and tile store located in the Dean building. Currently, the building is owned by Engles Furniture.

10. GORST & KING BUILDING

2079 Sherman Avenue

Charles O. King of Gorst & King, Inc., bus and jitney operators, announced plans in April 1923 to build a large modern concrete garage, office building and passenger depot. Vern C. Gorst, King and Milas Richardson had organized in 1912 to run a Marshfield-North Bend Auto Line. Their business grew in routes run, people carried and garage services offered.

Since 1915 the firm had rented the Terminal Garage at the north west corner of Sheridan and Virginia. However, their bus stop was on the east side

Sunrise Garage in the 1940s.
Courtesy Coos Historical and Maritime Museum.

Gorst & King building, center, after construction but before marquee attached.

22

Gorst & King's new orange and yellow Reo bus. Cost $5,200 with cane lined seats finished in walnut. *Coos Bay Harbor* April 4, 1924. Courtesy North Bend Public Library.

Tokens good for Englewood or Marshfield-North Bend routes.

of the 2000 block of Sherman Avenue where they had an office in the North Bend Newsstand. The April 1923 anouncement ended the company's many years wait for suitable conditions. In late 1919 they purchased Carl Albright's 35' x 100' lot with frontage on both Sherman and Sheridan, but chose not to build until material prices fell. They also wanted the adjoining corner lot, Sherman and Washington, but it wasn't available. (In 1922 this lot sold to the Dean group who built a service station there.)

Now, in 1923, Gorst and King purchased the Backey Estate lot north of the lot they owned giving them a 70' frontage on Sherman, between the Gurnea Service Station and Palace Hotel.

William N. Able and his crew from Marshfield, finished excavating the site in October 1923 while Metzger and Iron, Roseburg, general contractors for the building's exterior also had men at work.

Thursday, February 28, 1924, the three-story building, its exterior finished in abalone stucco, was turned over to Gorst & King. Contracts for the interior had not yet been let. The total cost ran about $20,000.

The company's goal was to provide a comfortable facility for bus passengers, space for main offices, a sales room and general storage. They estimated they could house sixty cars. In September 1924 the largest and costliest marquee in the county was fitted on the Gorst and King Building. It extended the width of the structure and overhung the sidewalk to give shelter from the elements.

The firm noted that the building was too large for present needs, but they looked ahead to completion of the Roosevelt Highway (101) when they would be the terminus for buses running both north and south. Gorst and King ran busses from this location until 1964. Their motto: "Better Public Service."

Engles Furniture now owns the building.

Building with marquee. Courtesy Coos Historical and Maritime Museum.

23

11. COOS BAY GOWN SHOP

2051 Sherman Avenue

Mrs. Charles (Cora) Hoyez moved her Coos Bay Gown Shop to 2051 Sherman in 1939 and in the early 1940s replaced the old wooden building with a one story, plus basement, fireproof concrete block building. The business office was in the back on the left, the alteration room toward the back on the right. The windows are as they were. The business remained at this address until closed in 1964.

In August 1931, with $50 and a sewing machine, Cora Hoyez had first opened a dress and gown making shop at 2066 Sherman (formerly Ralph's Café.) Mrs. Cecil L. Brown assisted. They carried a line of samples from the Hub in Marshfield, but no materials. Their slogan was "sewing North Bend high school uniforms a

Gown Shop sign at night. Image from the 1950s.

specialty."

The shop moved to a larger location at 1921 Sherman in March 1932. (Between Ryan's Grocery and Wilkinson's Store.) In 1937, the Gown Shop acquired Ruth's Stitch Shop and relocated there, south of Safeway on Sherman Avenue, its last stop before 2051 Sherman.

Mrs. Hoyez died in 1950. Her four daughters, Lillian, Leona, Laura and LaVerne Viola, carried on the business. Leona served as manager for many years. They were proud to carry Jonathon Logan dresses as well as other high quality apparel for women and children. For many years the Eastern Star purchased their gowns at the Coos Bay Gown Shop. The Hub in Marshfield was their main competitor. Friendly competition also came from The White House, located in North Bend's I.O.O.F. building.

The rise of Pony Village Mall doomed the Gown Shop. For some years after, a Moose Lodge located here. In 1997 Steve Simpkins purchased the building and moved his Yesterday's Books to the site.

Gown Shop building, now Yesterday's books, in 2005.

12. BURMESTER-FACKLER BUILDING

2072-2082 Sherman Avenue

Dr. H. E. Burmester practiced dentistry for many years from an office in the Winsor Building. H. J. Fackler owned a real estate and insurance business. Together, they invested in several North Bend properties.

In March 1924 the two men purchased a lot on Sherman Avenue, which the *Coos Bay Harbor* identified as next to Dad Radcliff's confectionery. In April the *Harbor* reported they had purchased a lot adjacent to their property on Sherman, just south of the Bock building. This gave them a 60' frontage and a 100' depth. They immediately planned a new concrete building.

The plan, drawn by architect A. L. Finley, allowed four storefronts - wider fronts on each end and two narrower in the center. Ted Halstead, a local contractor, built the one story building. G. A Perkins did the excavating, E. J. Arms the electrical work, and Reberg-Davis supplied all the hardware, plate glass, and sash and doors. Scaife & Hodgins (Marshfield) handled the painting. Schroeder & Hildebrand (Marshfield) did the plumbing and R. A. Corthell (Marshfield) the roof. The building's walls were double thick so that a second story (never done) could be added. Work was completed in late July 1924 for an estimated cost of $15,000.

The building opened fully occupied. Businesses, starting on the south and working north, were W. E. Bowles Grocery (2082 Sherman), Henry & Zastro beauty parlor and barber shop, Bergen the Florist, and Belding and Bushong (2072 Sherman) photography supplies, art goods and picture framing. Belding handled jewelry, also.

The Bowles Grocery planned to open August 2, promising to be:

BEST store in the
 BEST building on the
  BEST street in the
   BEST city in the
    BEST county in the
     BEST state in the
      BEST country in the whole world.

Unfortunately, real life did not square with unabashed boosterism. Store supplies were delayed and the opening was postponed. Customers did not prove plentiful and in February 1925 the Bowles Grocery stock was sold by court order.

In late 1925 H. J. Fackler sold his real estate/insurance business and moved to San Diego. Dr. Burmester, who came to North Bend in 1905, continued his dentistry practice and when Keizer Hospital opened in 1923 moved his office there. Burmester served several years on city council and as mayor of

Burmester-Fackler Building when new. *Coos Bay Harbor* of June 25, 1924. Image courtesy North Bend Public Library.

North Bend 1927-28. He died at his Sheridan Avenue home in April 1936.

The Burmester-Fackler Building became the Sundbaum Building when Sundbaum Shoes located there in 1927. In 2005 Christophe of Café 2000 owns the building and occupies three of its fronts. The fourth, 2082 Sherman, is rented.

13. KOLTES BUILDING

2000 Sherman Avenue

During the depression, the owner(s) of the Koltes Building decided on a bold move, perhaps because a potential lease was in hand. In June 1932 they tore down the one-story wooden building at the south west corner of Virginia and Sherman and replaced it with a modern one.

An August *Coos Bay Harbor* reported that the new

Dunham's Grocery in the concrete Koltes Building, circa 1932. Courtesy Coos Historical and Maritime Museum.

40' x 70' concrete Koltes building was nearly finished. The structure was leased to Dunham's Grocery, a firm that had been in North Bend since 1920 and called itself "Coos County's Own Stores."

Dunham's opened Saturday, September 17, 1932, with a splash. Inaugural specials included ten pounds of sugar for 19c at 9 a.m., ten bars of crystal white soap for 9c at 11 a.m., and ten cans of Alpine milk for 19c at 2 p.m. At 3 o'clock there were balloons containing coupons worth from $2 to $15. Toy washing machines, cedar chests and a Kiddie Kar were given away during the day. At 8:30 p.m. there was a beauty contest – a big $2.00 cake awarded to the loveliest woman present. "Competent judges will decide." Low prices were pledged as everything was on the self-service plan. Fourier's of Central Market in Marshfield, having recently purchased the Tupper Meat Market, ran the meat counter at Dunham's.

In August 1935 Dunham's Grocery sold out. Western States purchased its wholesale side and Safeway took the retail stores. So in 1935 the Koltes Building became identified as Safeway. (Safeway had come to North Bend in January 1932, first located at 2028 Sherman.) The concrete Koltes building had not used all its available lot. In 1939 a 30' x 40' addition extended the building west along Virginia.

Safeway stayed at the Koltes site until 1955, building a larger market west of McPherson, on the north side of Virginia. Dallas Troutman then occupied the old Safeway store, starting his Emporium, the flagship for what became a regional chain. Currently, the building houses American Furniture and the *South Coast Shopper*.

14. LOWERY APARTMENTS

1010 Virginia Avenue

Robert Lowery, Southern Pacific's ticket agent in North Bend and recent arrival to the city, bought George Witte's 95' x 100' lot on the north west corner of Virginia and Meade Avenues in October 1922. The sale price was $16,000. Lowery let a contract for an apartment building as soon as local architect, Fred Magnusson, finished the plans. North Bend had a housing shortage and not all who wanted to live in the city could.

Hamlin and Fry received a $8,816 general construction contract in November 1922. Plumbing, heating, wiring and painting were not included. Apartment interiors were plastered, the exterior done in stucco. The building was 47' x 49.5' with two stories and full basement. It had four three-room and four two-room apartments. Each had hot water radiators heating every room. The first steam heating system came from the Simpson/Myers building. When the latter was torn down for the new I.O.O.F. building, the heating plant was bought and moved to the apartments.

The building, known initially as the Lowery Apartments, was ready for occupants in April 1923. Dennis and Gertrude Hull - he managed the Liberty Theater - were the first tenants in apartment number one. In 1924 Largo and Stella Cutlip lived in number five. The Lowerys also had an apartment.

The Lowerys left the area in 1927 and Robert Lowery died in Stockton, California in 1931. Based on newspaper reports, we surmise George Witte retained a financial interest in the apartments and Lowery sold out to him when he left North Bend. Witte also died in 1931. A few months after her husband's death, Mrs. Witte sold the apartment building to Ivy Condron for cash.

Virgina Avenue Apartments, formerly Lowery Apartments. 2005 photo.

15. KEIZER HOSPITAL

Virginia Avenue at McPherson

In late 1919 Dr. Phil J. Keizer and brother Dr. Russell C. Keizer announced their joint practice and expectation to build a "modern, fire proof and strictly up to date hospital" for North Bend. They would specialize in surgery.

June 30, 1922, the *Coos Bay Harbor* headlined a $50,000 hospital building. The city sold lots to the Keizer brothers for $2500, the amount of street assessments and taxes due. Local architect, Fred Magnusson, drew plans for a 50' x 90' two-story concrete building with a full basement. Pat Tulley was the general contractor. Ira Padrick broke ground for the twelve feet deep basement early in July. (The county used the excavated dirt for fill near the Virginia Street Bridge.) A. J. Eberhardt did the plumbing and Marshfield Electrical Company installed the 20,000 plus feet of wire in the building. Skaife and Hedges had responsibility for painting while Padrick and Glazier provided the carpets and furnishings. Nurse, Miss Bertha Schmid, was named superintendent of the hospital.

When the hospital opened, February 4, 1923, its cost had reached $60,000. The basement housed a modern heating plant (janitor's quarters close by) and a kitchen with dumb waiter to carry food to the floors above. Nurses' quarters - bedrooms, bath and dining room - were also here, as was a large emergency room accommodating twelve beds. An elevator ran from the basement to all floors.

The first floor had a carpeted reception room, furnished in mahogany in Queen Anne style. Dr. Burmester, dentist, had a suite, as did the Keizer brothers. Directly behind reception were consulting and examining rooms. Dr. Ira Bartle, longtime North Bend practitioner, returned from Arizona to join the staff and received patients here. X-ray, dark room, stock rooms, and lavatories were also on this floor. On the floor's west wing were six private rooms, each well lighted and equipped with closet, water and bath.

The top floor had wards (one for women the other for men), five more private rooms and the nursery. The surgeries (one for major and one for minor), made up the west wing of this floor. Between the operating rooms was the

Keizer Brothers Hospital 1923-1924, before addition to north. Courtesy Coos Historical and Maritime Museum.

sterilization room with an electrically heated high pressure Wilmot Castle Sterilizer for surgical dressings, pans, equipment, etc. The doctors also used a specially built water sterilizer to wash-up before surgery.

On April 13, 1923, the *Harbor* noted that all the rooms in the new hospital were full and that Miss Schmid was an able manager. Virtually every nurse was named, including Mrs. Carol C. Hons, head nurse, and Miss M. D. Abercromble, the surgical nurse. The work of Mrs. Carl Wermark, cook, and Miss Inez Kjelland, secretary, was commended. Ed Moore the bookkeeper, and Arthur Whereat, the janitor, were also praised.

Keizer Brothers Hospital, Incorporated, announced in May 1923 that about $20,000 in stock would be sold to fund improvements. The brothers held a majority of the stock, while Dr. Bartle and Miss Schmid also held blocks. Certainly, throughout 1923, the hospital ran full or nearly so. In early 1924, banker, Harry Wenderoth (married to the Keizer brothers' sister Grace) came from Salem to be the hospital's business manager. He, too, had a share in ownership. The hospital was a private for profit institution but the stated practice of the owners was that no one would be turned away for lack of funds.

An expansion of the hospital was announced in June 1924. A northern annex gave the facility much needed space. Keizer Brothers had to do some horse trading to acquire the adjacent lot. First they bought J. A. Allen's vacant lot (next to the Pioneer Building in the 1800 block of Sherman) then traded it to the owner of the lot north of the hospital. Additional lots were also acquired.

Pat Tulley was again contractor for the $50,000 two-story concrete addition. When the new wing opened in January 1925, the hospital's floor space was doubled and the building's footprint a 90' x 90' square. The new basement was arranged for nurses quarters and a nurses training school. Part of the new first floor had more offices for staff added in the past year. Thirty-five new rooms were created. The combined wings handled 80 to 100 patients. Twenty rooms were private. The new nursery accommodated twelve babies.

In 1953 control of Keizer Hospital went to a non-profit group. The hospital was expanded again, in 1954, also to the north. New surgeries were built and the en-

Another view of Keizer Hospital in the 1920s. Courtesy Coos Historical and Maritime Museum.

trance changed from Virginia Avenue to McPherson. About $100,000 was spent in improvements. Keizer Hospital closed in May 1974 when the new Bay Area Hospital replaced smaller facilities in both North Bend and Coos Bay.

The men behind this hospital came to North Bend before and after World War I. Dr. Phil J. Keizer earned his medical degree before his older brother Russell and began his medical practice in North Bend in 1914 from an office in the Winsor building. When the United States joined World War I, Phil entered the Army Medical Corps as a lieutenant and rose to major. In September 1918 he was erroneously reported killed in France. At the war's end, he returned to North Bend. He kept the death certificate framed in his office. Patients were told "Hell, you can see I'm not dead." In January 1920 his brother Russell joined him. Russell

was a 1918 graduate of the University of Oregon medical college.

Dr. Russell Keizer and his wife had three children. In 1935 son Ennis had his medical degree, practicing at Keizer Hospital while son John was earning all A's at the University of Oregon's Portland medical school. As a reward for those A's dad gave him a new Dodge coupe. The Keizer's daughter was Mrs. Dale Hansen of Marshfield.

Dr. Russell Keizer died of a stroke in early November 1936. He was fifty-two years old. Seven years earlier, in October 1929, the other founder of the hospital, Dr. Phil Keizer, died at age forty-three.

16. HOTEL NORTH BEND
Sherman Avenue at Virginia

In January 1921 stockholders of the First National Bank of North Bend authorized construction of a new hotel. All previous hotels were wooden structures, many more appropriately called rooming houses. In March 1921 the bank directors voted unanimously for a modern fireproof hotel with dining room and all the latest fixtures. The expected cost for a three or four story building was $100,000. The bank intended to sell its "Brick Block" on Virginia at Sheridan and move to the new facility.

J. E. Tourtellotte, of Tourtellotte and Hummel Portland architects, however, proposed a five-story concrete building, to take advantage of the light and scenic view. He suggested sixty-four rooms, with fifty-two having private bath or shower. Tourtellotte planned the hotel entrance on Virginia and a fine fireplace in the lobby.

16-318 Keizer Bros Hospital – North Bend, Ore.

Keizer Hospital circa 1940. Expansion on the north visible to the right.

In early June North Bend Fuel and Transfer began excavating around the wooden Bank of Oregon building, housing the Daily pool hall and the North Bend Newsstand downstairs, and the telephone company upstairs. The old structure was moved to the north east corner of Union and Virginia freeing the hotel site.

August 12, 1921, the *Coos Bay Harbor* reported Hedges & Huls of The Dalles received the general construction contract for a five story concrete hotel, with sixty-eight rooms – each with hot and cold water and a telephone. Charles D. Snyder got plumbing and heating, American Electric Works the wiring, and Portland Elevator Company the elevator. 'When price of the land, moving the old bank building, and architect's commission was added up, the hotel's price became $116,400.

The hotel building had 60' frontage on Sherman and 140' on Virginia. The basement housed the heating plant and storerooms. The kitchen entrance was on Union Avenue in the rear of the wooden building moved there. The bank's quarters on Sherman were 60' x 60' with a storefront facing Sherman as well. The bank could move into that space if more room was needed.

The hotel lobby was 40' x 60.'

Bank entrance on Sherman Ave. Late 1922 view from IOOF construction site. Courtesy Coos Historical and Maritime Museum.

The left doorway, just after entering the lobby, led to the one-story dining room between the concrete hotel and the old Bank of Oregon building. The dining room had three rows of tables in the center, each table for four. About the sides was a row of tables for two. The main floors in the bank, hotel lobby and dining room were mosaic tile, "practically indestructible and should last at least 100 years." The mezzanine had writing tables and chairs for guests' use. Ten rooms on each floor had private baths; seven north-facing rooms on each floor were without baths.

In October 1921, with the building progressing rapidly, the Board of Directors of the First National Bank of North Bend officially named the new structure Hotel North Bend. Solid leather rockers and easy chairs were purchased for the lobby. Upholstered wicker chairs were on the mezzanine. Rooms had matched furniture in walnut, mahogany and oak, with color schemes matching carpet and wall color. Including furnishings, the new cost estimate was $125,000.

In November, E. E. Cleaver, Pendleton, put the roof on and soon windows went in. The hotel's exterior was finished in pure white Portland cement. In January 1922, the eight-passenger elevator arrived as did the four foot high eagle that was placed over the entrance to the bank. Two months later Coos & Curry Telephone Co. announced they were installing a 100 line private switchboard in the hotel and telephones in the rooms could handle long distance.

On February 17, 1922, the *Harbor* reported a Hotel North Bend lease to the Mills Brothers of Portland, described as "prominent and successful hotel men of Oregon." In mid-April 1922 the First National Bank of North Bend opened. President Henry G. Kern gave cut flowers to all the women visiting the bank. Cigars were passed out to the men.

Wednesday, May 3, 1922, the Hotel North Bend opened with a celebratory $2.50 dinner sponsored by the Chamber of Commerce. (The April 28 *Harbor* ran the menu.) Fred Lockley of the *Oregon Journal* was

scheduled to speak. Other speakers included E. O. McCormac and John M. Scott with the Southern Pacific Railroad. The hotel served 380 people at three settings of its opening dinner. A dance followed the meal. All hotel rooms were booked. The hope for the hotel was that "The doors must never be closed."

The *Harbor's* May 5, 1922, cost update reached $165,000.

In November 1923 the bank directors authorized another $10,000 to complete the hotel's unfinished fifth floor, giving thirteen more rooms. Additionally, the old Bank of Oregon building now called the Annex, connected to the second floor of the hotel by a hallway, was remodeled to make seventeen rooms available. Used metal furniture was painted to resemble oak in the Annex. The Hotel North Bend turned people away, and even with the additions, management feared the space might not meet demand.

Hotel North Bend showing Virginia Avenue entrance as well as the Sherman Avenue side. Note the annex location (far left) and the restaurant windows mimicking the Hotel's ground floor.

Renamed Hotel Coos Bay with sign across the highway, post 1936.

A delightful early occupant of the hotel was clairvoyant Madame Hoyt. Her ad from the *Harbor* of December 5, 1924, (reprinted here) tells it all.

In January 1925 the Mills Brothers sold their lease on the building, as well as the fixtures and furnishings, to local managers. The leasees were M. S. Taylor, North Bend's school superintendent (future national radio broadcaster and author of "The Voice of Experience") as well as two Marshfield partners, Price Westover and L. A. Blanc. Taylor lived at the hotel as manager and optimistically predicted the job would not interfere with his school duties. However, the work proved too time consuming and at the end of the year Taylor turned management duties over to A. E. Keighley. Mrs. Keighley took charge of the dining room.

Other management changes occurred, the dining room was closed and reopened. In 1931 the hotel got a red, blue and green neon sign. The sign hung on the Sherman Avenue corner with the words "Hotel" vertical and "North" and "Bend," above and horizontal.

In February 1936 the hotel was refurbished top to bottom. Sixty-one rooms were re-papered and all wood repainted. Bathrooms were enameled. The lobby and mezzanine floors were redecorated and the kitchen repainted. That same month, the faltering First National Bank of North Bend was sold to Portland's First National Bank. In April, the bank sold the hotel.

Mrs. James Collier, of Powers, acquired the hotel for $50,000. James Collier quickly sold his logging equipment and joined his wife. In May 1936 the Colliers had the building painted white and also changed the name to the Hotel Coos Bay. In time, they added a neon Hotel Coos Bay sign that hung across Sherman Avenue. By claiming the Hotel Coos Bay name, the

Hotel lobby as it looked in the late 1930s. Courtesy Coos Historical and Maritime Museum.

Collier's beat a potential buyer of the Tioga building in Marshfield who wanted the Hotel Coos Bay name for that edifice.

Under the Colliers tenure the dining area was re-worked. Its Virginia Avenue front became a coffee shop (closed in May 1937) with seven booths and thirteen counter chairs. A street entrance was cut at the second window west of the lobby. The dining room was remade, with general dining in the northeast corner, opening into the grill.

In 1959 the building's name was changed to the North Bend Hotel. Decline, closing and dereliction followed. A non-profit group tried to run the building, but defaulted. A local oversight group picked up the pieces and worked to find a buyer. In 2004 Umpqua Community Development Corporation, Roseburg, acquired the hotel.

Umpqua's application for a National Register of Historic Places designation for the hotel was approved in August 2005. (North Bend's first building so honored). In the next two years the corporation plans to refurbish the building for mixed income housing. The community's most substantial building once again will be suitably outfitted for its prominent downtown corner. It will be called the Hotel North Bend once again.

Close up of Hotel marquee, mid 1940s.
Courtesy Pat Choat Pierce.

17. NORTH BEND CASH MARKET
1960 Sherman Avenue

Frank Muscus and Bill Reed opened their new 30' x 90' concrete building in June 1924. They purchased the property, occupied by F. W. Woods, Realtor, for $8,000. A wooden building was razed and Pat Tully built a structure designed specifically for a meat market. Previously the two men had operated their North Bend Cash Market from leased quarters in the Simpson/Myers building, 1979 Sherman Avenue.

The new building, as described in the *Coos Bay Harbor*, had an arcade front and full plate glass windows. The public shop area was 25' x 36', with marble counters. There were three cutting blocks. The showcases were equipped with cooling pipes to keep the meat fresh.

Adjacent to the shop was a 9' x 13' five ton capacity refrigerator, powered by a five horsepower electric motor. The refrigerator had a door leading to the meat cutting room. Next to the cutting room was the main 13' x 16' cooling room. The latter had five tracks each with a control switch to help in moving the beef quarters around. Twenty-five head of beef could be handled. A main track ran from the front of the building down a hallway to the refrigerator and cooling rooms.

A kitchen for lard rendering, sausage cutting and meat grinding was located in the rear. A six horsepower boiler furnished steam to operate the machines. All rooms had concrete floors and drains in order to increase sanitation.

Even before the national depression, the Cash Market had moved across the street to 1937 Sherman.

The Cash Market building as it appeared in the 1940s. Courtesy Coos Historical and Maritime Museum.

The depression apparently affected Frank and Bill's business plans. In 1932, for example, they reported a loss on a load of cattle sent to market in Portland. By Easter time 1936 they advertised meat and poultry as available from their North Bend Packing Company located once again in rented space in the I.O.O.F. building, 1979 Sherman.

Frank Muscus was a North Bend council member from 1935 until 1947.

Coos Head Food Cooperative has owned the building at 1960 Sherman since 1973.

18. I.O.O.F. BUILDING
Sherman Avenue at Virginia

August 1922 the Arago Lodge, International Order of Odd Fellows, took over the circa 1906 two story frame Simpson/Myers building from the Simpson Estate Company. In return for their property valued at $25,000, the Estate Company took the I.O.O.F.'s $10,000 frame building (two lots north) plus $15,000 in stock.

The Odd Fellows proposed a new three-story fire proof building on the 100' x 100' lot. Fred Hollister was charged with securing a $35,000 loan and a committee was formed to raise at least $8,000 from the general public.

By mid-October 1922 Lorsung & Son, Marshfield, contracted to remove the old Simpson building within thirty days. The contractor got all materials, glass, doors, windows, plumbing, heating plant, etc. and paid $200 in addition. Within three weeks the job was done and the fire department burned the remaining rubbish.

Preliminary plans submitted by J. E. Tourtellotte, Portland architect, were accepted by the I.O.O.F. By mid-December construction contracts went to area businesses. M. W. Payne was general contractor with a $43,848 bid. Charles D. Snyder got the heating bid for $3,840, A. J. Eberhardt the plumbing at $2002 and Marshfield Electric Co. the wiring for $547.

Architect Tourtellotte received a six-percent commission, some $3,000. Total cost for the site and construction was about $78,200. The contract required the building be finished by June 1, 1923, but the main lodge hall had to be available by May 10. That gave the

(continued on page 38)

MAP OF BUILDINGS AND SITES COVERED

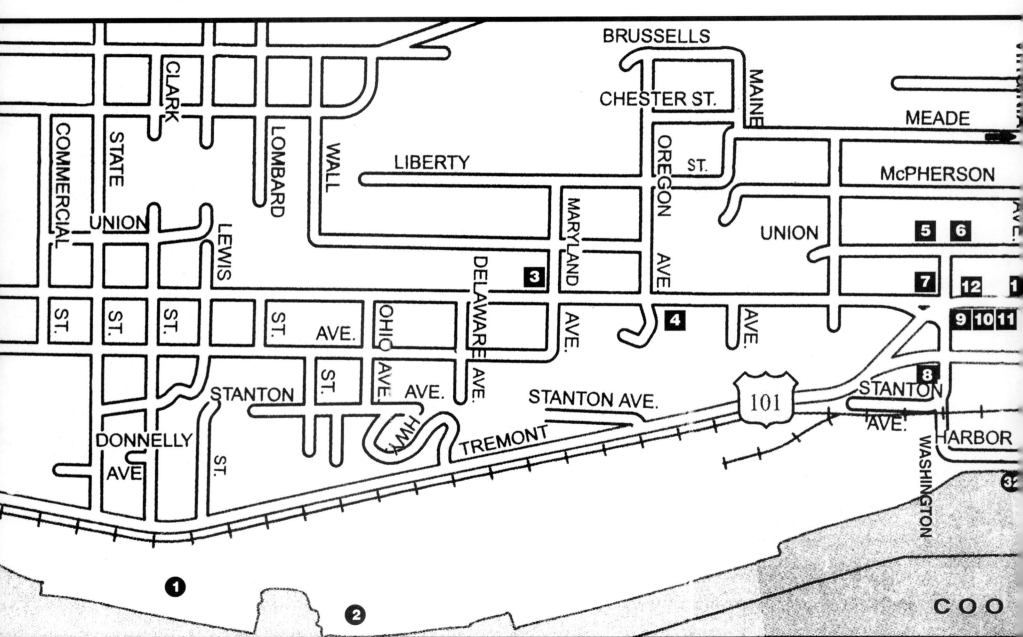

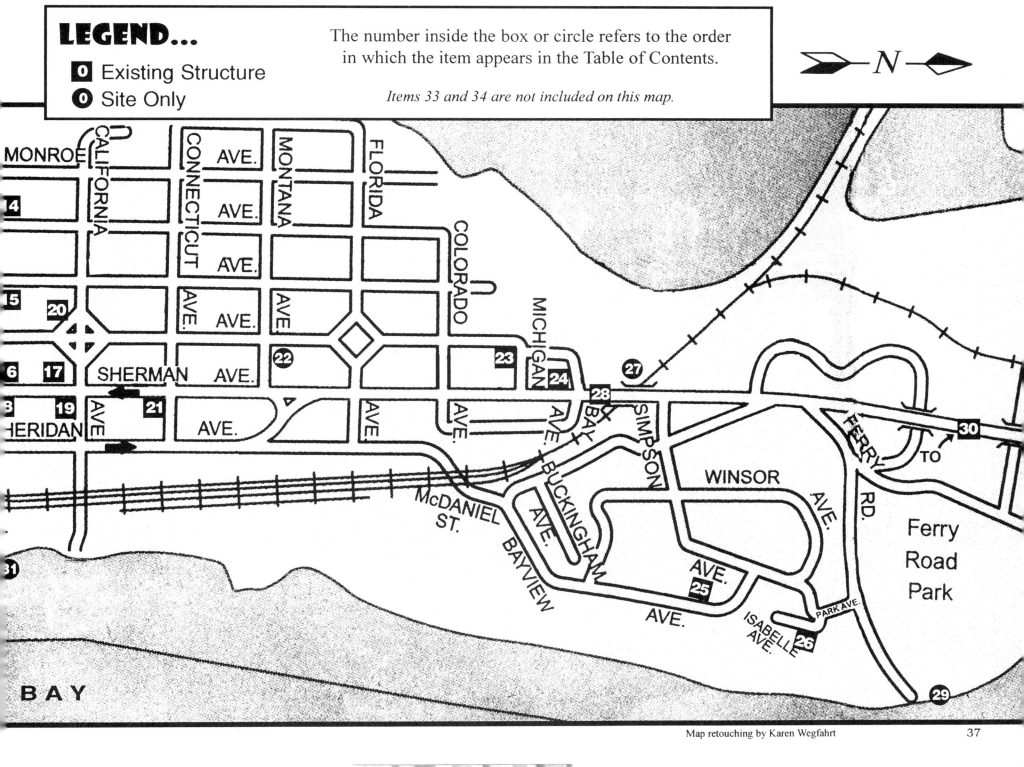

I.O.O.F. time to prepare for hosting the state meeting of their Grand Lodge May 21-24.

The building, with a full basement was designed for multiple uses. The main floor was divided for lease to a "better quality" of stores. The second and third floors were for offices and apartments all arranged to have outside views. Lodge rooms and auditorium, on the second and third floors, were on the inside of the building. The entire building was heated by steam and all the plumbing pipes were made of brass. Come late January 1923, workers were ready to pour the concrete first floor. Timbers for the second story had been raised and the public was assured a number of these beams were more substantial than usually seen. The 95' by 100' building was mostly complete by mid-May. The exterior was painted white and only interior details remained undone.

Four of the building's five large storefronts on Sherman Avenue had already been leased. The southern corner and basement was taken by Padrick & Glazier Furniture Co., the next space by C. L. Brown's Economy Store, then Mrs. A. J. Davis' White House

store and finally Allen and Curl's grocery. (The Allen & Curl grocery became Allen & Co. in May 1924 as Curl sold out. J. A. Allen shortly sold out in September to Twentieth Century Grocers, a chain.)

Second floor frontage on Sherman was filled by Dr. T. F. Mongomery, dentist, Robertson Land Company and a suite of rooms for attorneys Fred Hollister, Fred Bynom and Judge Hammond.

In 1924 Prof. R. G. White used the top floor of the I.O.O.F. building for his Coos Bay Business College. He resigned as North Bend High School principal to give full time to the college.

In September 1930, after selling her house, a widowed Mrs. Fred Hollister moved into the top floor of the I.O.O.F. building. Here, as in her home, she rented rooms to teachers. She located the Hollister Insurance office on the second floor. In March of 1933 the White House store moved from its central room to the Sherman Avenue corner of the building. It became one of the longest tenants in the building.

Currently California interests own the building. Pirate's Cove has occupied the northern storefront for years. Small businesses rent the other fronts with residential space continuing above.

I.O.O.F. Building as construction finished in 1923.

19. RUSH BUILDING

1901 Sherman Avenue

The (Bert) Rush building likely dates to an earlier era, but our first specific identification of it was found in 1922 when the building was leased to J. F. Weatherly for five years. Weatherly's intent was to make the Sherman Avenue frontage a butcher shop and the California Avenue space a wholesale ice cream operation.

John Beck came to North Bend from Washington state in 1924, purchasing the Leader Bakery (1879 Sherman) from William Schneider.

In May 1935 Beck bought the Rush Building, south east corner of Sherman and California, from George Dieppe. Beck wanted to expand his business. He now had a bakery next door at 1903 Sherman, in a building he had built in 1927. The latter was to be used exclusively for the preparation and baking of various breads sold locally and in the valley. The new purchase would be his retail store.

Mr. Thielman was in charge of remodeling the Rush building. A new front and new hardwood floors were put in the retail shop. A center room became the

Rush building as the Day Bakery before remodeling. *Coos Bay Harbor* image, August 4, 1949. Courtesy North Bend Public Library.

pastry shop while the rear of the building housed wrapping and loading activities.

In December 1938 Beck sold the bakery business and equipment to Frank Day (Eugene) and Linton Benson (Salem) for about $25,000. The purchasers were both experienced in the trade. Day took up residence locally and the bakery operated under the name Day's Bakery. Mr. Beck kept the buildings, renting them. Summer 1949 Day's Bakery building got a facelift. The second story was removed and both the interior and exterior redecorated.

(During the 1930s it was common knowledge that the second floor of the Rush building sheltered a bawdyhouse. At least one young local coal deliveryman regretted that his boss wouldn't let him trade coal for services.)

In 1986 the building was the last location of the *North Bend News* (titled *Coos Bay Harbor* before 1951.) Presently, it is home to the Crystal Dolphin Gallery.

Site for new city hall. Image from *Coos Bay Harbor*,
January 26, 1939. Courtesy North Bend Public Library.

20. CITY HALL

California Avenue at Union

In 1923 J. E. Tourtellotte designed a new Marshfield City Hall on Central Avenue. Marshfield's new
structure made North Bend's old 1906 wooden building
absolutely dismal by comparison. (North Bend's City Hall
was outdated by 1914 when Mayor Simpson declared it
"neither a credit to the city or up to the standard of ne-
cessity.")

There were occasional bursts of interest in replacing city hall, but nothing happened during the depression. Then in 1938 a federal public works project was
approved for a North Bend City Hall.

The *Coos Bay Harbor* reported on August 4, 1938,
that the city council had decided to go ahead. Council
wanted to limit the cost to $30,000 with the govern-
ment purchasing the 55% overlap bond while 45% of
the cost would be a gift from the Works Progress Administration. Francis B. Jacobberger, Portland architect, designed the building to house offices, council
chambers, library and fire department. His design also
included several structural options (not used) such as a
jail and a second story office penthouse.

Tom Lillebo of Reedsport got the contract for the
new hall to be built north of Keizer Hospital, on California between Union and McPherson. George Melville had
the plumbing contract. The foundation of the brick
building was concrete. The basement had a boiler room
for the oil furnace and other trappings that supplied
hot water to the building's radiators. Room was also al-
located for archives and a vault.

On March 23, 1939, the *Harbor* noted that the
lumber supporting the concrete walls on the ground
floor had been removed, window casings were in and all
rooms had temporary floors. With good weather aiding,
the concrete was soon waterproofed. An estimated
25,000 bricks, both cream and medium brown, began
to arrive. The bricks were alternated to give a pleasing
appearance. Bob Huggins and Anton Jensen were the
bricklayers.

The second story of the building was for the firemen's use. There was a kitchen, shower room and
sleeping space. A chute gave the men fast access to
their equipment housed in the main floor wing facing
Union Avenue. The wing had three large doors, which
swung up and out of the way, so the fire engines could
exit quickly.

In April 1939 the council considered $800 suffi-
cient to furnish the chairs, desks, file cabinets and

other office equipment needed for the building. In May the concrete walkways and driveways were laid, including a 40' x 60' area from the fire department's doors to the street.

Directly off the main entrance lobby was the office shared by the recorder and the treasurer. Immediately south of the recorder's office were the two rooms used by the city engineer. The police department also had two rooms on the south side of the building. The council chamber was on the north side of the building.

Mayor Largo Cutlip accepted the brick structure on July 6, 1939. At the July 15th dedication of the $40,000 building, officials from all levels of government were present. All North Bend city officials, including police and fire, were there as well as Mayor J. Stanley Emery of Marshfield and Mayor George Melville of Empire. W.P.A. and state officials were also on hand. L. J. Simpson addressed the crowd of 600 spectators (*Harbor* count, *Coos Bay Times* count 300). Simpson spoke of the early days of North Bend - a subject he knew so very well - the flag was raised and the high school band, directed by George Payson, played.

The 1939 structure enlarged, upgraded, and functional still houses North Bend city government. The North Bend library occupied a McPherson Avenue wing from 1953-1989. In 1965 the fire department moved to a new building across the street on McPherson. The police department took over the vacated space.

City Hall as it appeared in the mid 1950s. Left, the fire department's open doors. Courtesy City of North Bend.

21. KERN BUILDING
1805 Sherman Avenue

In late 1923 Ira Padrick excavated the basement for a 60' x 100' two-story concrete garage on the site of the old wooden Hotel North Bend, south east corner of Sherman and Connecticut Avenues. The hotel burned in 1911 and the space remained vacant for a dozen years. The new building, to be called the Coos Garage, was a venture of Henry G. Kern, owner of the North Bend Iron Works.

Ted Halstead super-

Henry Kern. Courtesy Coos Historical and Maritime Museum.

Buick ad from *Coos Bay Harbor*, April 4, 1924. Jennings ad next page from *Coos Bay Harbor*, December 10, 1926. Courtesy North Bend Public Library.

vised construction of the estimated $20,000 Coos Garage structure. Fred V. Forbes, the White truck dealer, and T. Ben Currie, the Buick auto salesman, moved in from their sales location in the Gurnea Service Station. (See the Buick ad placed in the *Coos Bay Harbor*.) Due to the lot's slope, the basement floor was entered from the rear, while the second floor was level with Sherman Avenue.

In December 1926 Jennings Motor Company, Essex & Hudson dealers, occupied the building for a short time. By December 1927, A. M. Peterson, located at Union & Connecticut since early 1926, took a long-term lease and moved his Peterson Funeral Home into the already remodeled quarters.

The building's 6000 square foot main floor was arranged into special use areas for the funeral home. The entrance lobby and reception room led to a chapel that sat 400. There was a music room, two "slumber" rooms, an office and ladies and gentlemen's rest rooms. The preparation room was 12' x 24' and the casket showroom 24' x 36'. The 67' x 22' indoor parking space accommodated twelve to fifteen cars. The funeral home remained in the Kern building until September 1930 when Peterson built a mortuary adjacent to the Hollister house on McPherson Avenue at Virginia.

In mid-1932 Carl Golder leased the Kern building for his expanding auto parts store. He stayed until he acquired the American Legion Hall in 1934.

August 1935 the Kern Building hosted the North Bend Flower Show. Mrs. John Beck, of Beck's Bakery, was general chairman. In November 1936 Henry Kern had the building remodeled again so that it could be rented as a service station. The glass front was removed and concrete cut from the north and south walls to make vehicle entrances.

A gas station was in the building in the early 1940s and since the late 1940s North Bend Body Shop has occupied the building.

Henry Kern was a stalwart and active citizen. Born in 1875 and a Spanish American War veteran, Kern established the North Bend Iron Works in 1904. The waterfront business had a rough few years and early backers dropped out, L. J. Simpson buying their stock. In 1908 Simpson sold it all to Kern for just what he had in it. Kern was always a strong Simpson supporter.

Kern was appointed to a city council term in 1910 and served until 1918. That same year he was appointed mayor when E. F. Russell resigned. Kern served until 1921. In the 1920s, Kern was a county commissioner, a president of the First National Bank and a member of the North Bend School Board.

North Bend Body Shop, formerly Kern building, Connecticut Avenue side, looking south. 2005 image. Original site of North Bend's first hotel built in 1903.

H. G. Kern, President of the First National Bank of North Bend, signed this National Currency $10 note. See lower right hand corner for his actual inked signature.

22. COMMUNITY BUILDING

Montana Avenue at Union

The need for a community building for concerts, lectures, Chautauqua programs and a gymnasium grew after the pavilion in City Park was dismantled in 1923. North Bend voters in 1922 approved by one vote a $30,000 bond for a building but the city council disliked the plans presented and refused to authorize construction. The American Legion then tried promoting the concept, but without success. In late 1925 the Chamber of Commerce appointed a committee to spearhead the project. Action followed.

North Bend Community Building in the early 1960s. Courtesy Coos Historical and Maritime Museum.

In December 1925 the concrete foundation was poured for the frame Community Gymnasium as the building first was called. L. J. Simpson furnished the site, at the north east corner of Union and Montana, to the city. The city then gave the site, a 200' x 210' lot, to the Chamber of Commerce. The chamber's building committee was William Stout, Robert Banks and Henry G. Kern. Fred Magnusson donated the architectural plans. A. R. Helm and John Granstrom were in charge of construction. The building faced Montana, and other lots, already excavated (for the never built Hotel Simpson) were reserved for a future swimming pool.

The community building had wide approval, from the chamber of commerce and school board to the city council and civic organizations. A public subscription goal of $7,000 was set. A subscription form went to every resident of the city. Pledges ranged from $5 to $300.

Plans called for a 100' x 110' frame structure with a seating capacity of 1200 for basketball games, and 800 more floor seats when used as an auditorium. The gym had a twenty foot ceiling and the maple auditorium floor was 45' x 90'. A modern stage with the stage curtain illustrating Sunset Bay was installed. The building had four front rooms for women's groups and other organizational use.

The Community Building was dedicated on February 10, 1926. The fire department sponsored a dance and L. J. Simpson gave an address and presided over the ceremonies. The Marshfield Eagles closed their dance that night so that the Tower Dance Orchestra could play in North Bend.

In April the city council used the building for a reception for recently married Mayor Phil Keizer and his second wife. About 1,000 people attended and

L. J. Simpson gave the address of welcome.

When the building accounts were tallied in July 1926 some debt remained. Cost of the building, mostly labor, was $11,375. Cash collected was $4896, labor and materials donated $2,299, leaving a loan/debt of $4,300. With community unemployment growing, payment of the modest debt proved difficult.

Besides basketball, the building was used for Chautuaqua lecture series, flower shows, magicians and even showing a locally shot movie. "Sheikville Ranch," screened in late July 1930 with 50% of the gross benefiting the airport.

In 1934 and 1935 the "Negro Ghosts," the N. Y. Harlemites, played basketball here. In late July and into August 1935, the building hosted a Walkathon, drawing entrants from as far away as Michigan and Kansas. Contestants were on the floor forty-five minutes of each hour. Entertainment, from dancing to derby races, formed a part of the Walkathon. Local churches, the Women's Club and the Townsend Club opposed the latter activity.

When the Bandon fire destroyed much of that city in 1936, the North Bend Community Building was used as an assembly point for donations of help and shelter for refugees from the flames. The last high school basketball games here were in spring 1937, for in November of that year the new gym on the high school grounds was finished.

In 1941 the growth of the North Bend police reserves caused the city council to give the reserves the exclusive use of the Community Building. The building was used for whatever the situation required. The Community Building survived until the early 1960s.

23. LYLE B. CHAPPELL HOUSE
1405 Union Avenue

On July 31, 1925, the *Coos Bay Harbor* reported that Lyle and Fern Chappell were building a modern stucco house at the corner of Union and Michigan Avenues. The site was in the Ball Park Addition, the original North Bend ball field. The home sits approximately where the grandstands were. The 40' x 100' lot was purchased for $400 plus $1,000 in street and sewer assessments. The house was built for $5,000.

Lyle Chappell. Courtesy Coos Historical and Maritime Museum.

The Chappells drew their own plans, engaging Walter Livengood as chief carpenter at $12.00 a day. Assisting carpenters, at $8.00 per day each, were Dick Fry and Lou Gardiner. George Perkins excavated for the basement and foundation. Vincent Arrington did the concrete foundation. Cal Langworthy handled the electrical wiring, Schroeder and Hildebrand the plumbing while Chris Miller and Charles Kaiser did the plastering and stucco.

The Chappells moved into their home in late October 1925. Upon entering the house, there was a full width living room. On the left (north) beyond was the breakfast room, a kitchen and laundry. The bath was centered at the back. On the right (south) were two bedrooms and stairs up to an open attic, later partitioned, as well as stairs down to the half basement. The bedroom closets were built out from the south wall. Originally, a wood range and fireplace provided the home's heat. Later a furnace was added in the basement. The kitchen and dining room were remodeled in 1960. In 1967 an 8' x 16' addition was added to the back.

Lyle Chappell (1894-1985) had a remarkable life. He was born in Michigan and came to North Bend as a young man in 1906. His father, William, had come west in 1899 and called his family to Oregon in 1900. The family lived in Eugene prior to moving to North Bend. In North Bend, the Chappell family lived in the second home built in Bangor.

In June 1908 William Chappell (his wife and two youngest of their four sons out of town visiting relatives back in Michigan) became a foreman for J. G. Horn who contacted to build the Simpsons' Shore Acres home. Lyle, his brother Murlin, their father and a boarder moved by horse and wagon to the site. For the next three months they lived in a tent where, while his father worked on construction, Lyle cooked and cleaned for the occupants of the tent. (Years later, in the summer of 1916 or 1917, Lyle returned to Shore Acres, working on L. J. Simpson's farm.)

On Saturday night, June 27, 1914, Lyle rode with young Henry Kern in an Overland auto held up by highwaymen on the Empire road, about one-half mile south of Bangor, near Empire Lakes. Two black-masked robbers, carrying a shotgun, stopped five autos between 10 p.m and 2 a.m. Victims, hands over heads, lost their money, watches, and jewelry. As Lyle, without money or watch, turned over his billfold containing personal effects, a familiar voice said, "I don't want any of your personal effects, Lyle." The voice was that of Claude Allen. The other was Ed Wilson, later a bootlegger. The robbers were never found out (at the time) or punished. These two Bangor neighbors allegedly stole wood from the Chappell cellar as well as canned fruit and vegetables from Mrs. Chappell's basement cupboard.

Lyle excelled at debate during high school (1913 graduate) and his former forensic coach, Mrs. Birdie Clark, invited him to teach at Quincy, Oregon. Lyle took the required exam, passed and got a one-year teaching

Chappell home. Courtesy Marie Chappell Martin.

certificate. In September 1914 he was assigned the 4th, 5th and 6th grades. That year he fractured his left elbow that, while set, never again moved properly. He became principal of the Quincy school in fall 1916. After the 1918 school term, he thought of quitting teaching as wages in other professions rose so much more. Instead, in late June, he went off to war, though as the *Harbor* put it, "his left arm is not much use." Lyle volunteered for the new "limited service" option for men with minor defects who had previously been rejected. After the 1919 armistice, Lyle got a job at Beaver Hill School. Then he met Fern Evelyn DeLong (1897-1997) of Four Mile. He proposed in June 1919 and in June 1921 he and Fern married. It was a love that lasted a lifetime. The Chappells had two daughters, Lucille and Marie.

Lyle took and passed the post office civil service exam in 1919. North Bend Postmaster J. T. McGuire hired him in December 1919 at a salary of $100 per month. In January 1924 President Harding appointed Lyle Chappell, postmaster to succeed McGuire. In September 1924, Lyle announced that as of October 1 there would be free home delivery of mail - service twice daily to over 800 homes. Both Presidents Coolidge and Hoover kept Republican Chappell as postmaster. However in 1936, Franklin Roosevelt appointed Mrs. Fred Hollister to the job. Lyle returned to his civil service postal position and remained until retirement in 1953.

In addition to schoolteacher, World War I serviceman and postmaster, Lyle Chappell served in many public positions. He was an American Legion Commander, Kiwanis club member and president, Masonic Lodge member and Senior Grand Steward. When Lyle retired from the post office, the North Bend council immediately appointed him city recorder, treasurer and municipal judge, positions he held until 1962. He became a member of council (1962-1966) also serving as interim city manager for six months. Lyle Chappell was elected North Bend mayor for the 1966-68 term. During his council/mayor days he opposed two efforts to consolidate cities on the bay and wrote, "It appears that we as a City have something which someone else would like to have." Over his life he spoke about, shared in and embodied North Bend history. For many years he was fondly known as "Mr. North Bend."

24. DR. PHILIP J. KEIZER HOUSE
1410 Sherman Avenue

Dr. Phil Keizer. Courtesy of Norm and Eileen Bjarnson

In August 1922 with the lot cleared and excavation for the basement underway, architect Fred Magnusson was finalizing plans for Dr. Phil Keizer's "colonial type" house. The $5000 six or seven room house was built on the northerly of two lots Dr. Keizer bought just south of City Park. Contractors Laird and Arrington completed their work in March 1923. The new home was large enough to accommodate the doctor, his mother Mabel Keizer and stepfather John Keizer. (Dr. Keizer's sister Grace and her husband H. J. Wenderoth later built on the southern lot, 1418 Sherman).

Dr. Keizer remained single until 1926. (While in

Dr. Phil J. Keizer's house 1930's. Courtesty of Norm and Eileen Bjarnson. Below right side view 2005.

ding performed by Rev. J. E. Snyder. The Presbyterian minister redid the marriage vows "to remove any irregularities that might exist" in the Cleveland ceremony. Faux crippled and bandaged ushers, firemen and two small girls, Lea Rover and Patricia Mitchell, preceded the couple down the aisle. Ex-servicemen acted as bodyguards. School Superintendent M. S. Taylor played the wedding march. During the service the traffic warden arrested Rev. Snyder and at least one soul objected rather than forever holding his peace. The bride's special gift was a large rolling pin. Citizens gave the newlyweds a silver table service. Taylor recited an original poem that eulogized women and L. J. Simpson gave a humorous address. Attendees also enjoyed music, dancing and refreshments. After the reception firemen compelled the Keizers to ride the fire engine with siren screaming.

The Keizers lived in the North Sherman Avenue home. In 1928 they adopted a two-month old boy and named him Frank. Shortly they adopted a daughter, Catherine.

Dr. Phil Keizer served North Bend in many ways.

college he had married an "opera star" but divorced several years later. The couples' professional careers with long absences took them in separate directions). At the end of March 1926 in Cleveland, Ohio, Keizer married Bertha "Betty" Schmid, Superintendent of Keizer Hospital. She was in the east to attend a special course in anesthesia.

North Bend citizens did not let their popular mayor's quiet out of town marriage go unnoticed. In April about thirty people organized a very special reception at the new Community Building. The city was decorated with flags and there was a welcome banner. Chief Loomis and his fire department were in charge of decorations. Some 1000 people came for the mock wed-

In 1920 he was elected President of the North Bend Chamber of Commerce and served about four years in that post. In addition he was a Commander of the American Legion Post and a member of the Coos Bay Port Commission. Phil and brother, Russell, opened Keizer Hospital in 1923. From January 1923 to January 1927, Phil Keizer also served as mayor of North Bend.

Dr. Phil Keizer fought a liver cancer that claimed him in October 1929 at Good Samaritan Hospital, Portland. His funeral was held in Marshfield and he was buried at Sunset Cemetery. North Bend lost a giant.

The home remained in family hands until Bertha Keizer sold the house in 1985.

25. HACKETT HOUSE

1375 Bayview

The J. F. Hacketts moved from Hood River to North Bend and in April 1925 bought the Glazier & Padrick furniture business located in the Odd Fellows Building (I.O.O.F.)

By June 1926 the Hacketts had a two-bedroom English cottage style house almost completed in the new residential development of Simpson Heights. Oregon Home Designers, Portland, drew up the plans. The exterior simulated an English cottage in its steep rooflines, gables, casement windows, coarsely laid shingles and rough plaster. House plans included an ell as a potential addition.

Walter Livengood, carpenter, was the general contractor. Kaiser and Miller did the masonry, plaster and stucco; Victor M. Arrington, concrete; Coos Bay Electric, wiring; Robert Gebhardt, painting and tinting;

and A. J. Eberhart, plumbing. Hackett's own company laid the permanent linoleum floors used throughout the house. The latter were commended for their beauty and practicality.

The home's interior had all the necessities for modern living while retaining features such as an English style raised hearth fireplace and small balcony on the stair landing. A large view window faced the bay. When construction was complete, the Hacketts announced their "Home Beautiful" demonstration house open to the public starting Sunday, June 27, and at certain hours daily until July 3 - rather a smart move for someone in the furniture business. Hackett's stated aim was to reach people interested in building and fur-

Hackett house photo in *Coos Bay Harbor* June 25, 1926. Courtesy North Bend Public Library.

nishing moderately priced houses.

Portland had two representatives at the opening, Mr. Uppinghouse of Oregon Home Designers and Mr. Mulloy, Packard Mulloy Company, designers of the home's wrought iron lighting fixtures. Much attention focused on the use of color in decorating, with special mention of the draperies and brightly painted hanging bookshelves. The bathroom was done in mauve and pale green, the kitchen in yellow, black and red to suggest peasant (folk) art. At mid-week of the open house some furnishings changed to showcase different styles.

One can surmise the "House Beautiful" event was a business success. By early 1930 Hackett partnered with A. A. Ross of Astoria. The Ross-Hackett firm took over the North Bend store and acquired two more in Marshfield, Going Furniture Company and Johnson Furniture Company.

26. TOWER HOUSE
490 Isabelle Avenue

The stately Tudor style house with lovely well kept grounds sits on a bluff south of Ferry Road Park and affords a commanding view of the bay. The house, designed for Russ and Belle Tower by a Portland architect, replaced a home damaged by fire.

During a fierce windstorm in February 1920 sparks from the nearby Simpson mill set the house roof aflame. The house wasn't destroyed but the Towers razed it and started over. The English Tudor chosen was very popular after World War I. Many families of means adopted this style suggestive of an English country manor.

During the mid and late 1920s, the Simpson

Heights residential development grew west of the Tower house. While geographically related, the Tower property was not part of that development.

The Towers experienced some unexpected excitement during the Christmas season in 1936. They returned home one evening to find a burglar scooping up their valuables in a bag. The surprised intruder pulled out a gun, took a shot at Belle, missed and fled dropping his spoils. The villain was caught and the Towers expressed appreciation for the good police work.

Russ Tower died in 1971. Belle remained in the house until her death in 1986. The street on which the house sits was named for her.

Tower house from bay looking south in 2005

Some background adds significance to the Tower site. The original house (known as the "Old Town" house), built sometime in the last decades of the nineteenth century, was used by Captain A. M. Simpson while on the bay attending to his North Bend mill and shipyard. Summer 1899 it became newlywed L. J. and Cassie Simpson's first home. The house was a Simpson family gathering place and a center of early North Bend's social life. The house remained the Simpsons' in town winter home even after Shore Acres was built in 1908.

Isaac Russell (Russ) Tower and Mildred Isabelle (Belle) Stearns married in February 1918. (Belle was Cassie Simpson's daughter by her first husband.) L. J. and Cassie, who had been living at Shore Acres year round since 1914, gave their "Old Town" house to the young couple as a wedding gift.

27. AUTO CAMP IN CITY PARK

North Sherman Avenue

Cars were the rage, roads improved and large numbers of people were on the move. To accommodate tourists traveling by car, the North Bend Chamber of Commerce, in cooperation with North Bend's Park Committee, opened an auto camp in August 1921. The camp was located in the park at the end of Sherman Avenue just south of the railroad cut. (Sherman Avenue did not go through City Park until construction started on the big bridge in 1934). The camp setting, amidst acres of "primeval forest," included such amenities as cleared spaces, piped water, gas, telephone, electric lights, lavatories and a double size camp oven. Wood was supplied and there was a long table for communal

use. Caretaker, C. T. Fariss, lived on site to assist campers.

In March 1923 the chamber authorized a work crew under Ira Padrick's direction to help tear down the park pavilion built by the Simpson Lumber Company in 1902. Salvaged lumber was used to put up camp sheds and make other improvements. During the season the camp hosted over 3200 people in 677 vehicles.

The chamber's civic project had unintended consequences. By October 1923 community leaders took their concerns about "squatters" to the city council. The auto camp was closing for the season but an estimated thirty families had set up more permanent housekeeping. The Park Committee, backed by the council, or-

Auto camp, North Sherman Avenue. 1921 or 1922 photo before Keizer house built. House on left is just north of Keizer home location.
Courtesy Coos Historical and Maritime Museum.

dered all living quarters vacated at once. Their rationale was that in the absence of an established sewer system there was a "danger of pestilence." The park residents who had planned to winter over were very upset. Mayor Phil Keizer appealed to all city residents who had vacant property to list it with a realtor for rental.

Tuesday, April 15, 1924, was declared park day by the mayor and set aside for improving City Park. The primary project was to build a caretaker's bungalow at the park entrance. Those persons who couldn't come and work were asked to contribute to the Park Committee so skilled carpenters could be hired. Mr. Atwell, architect, donated the plans, Peter Loggie, plasterboard, Kruse and Banks, doors and frames, E. J. Arms, electrical work and the mills, some of the other materials. The cost of build-

ing supplies was estimated at $700.

In May 1925 the *Coos Bay Harbor* reported that the state board of health had issued rules and regulations regarding tourist campgrounds, both public and private. The rules covered water supplies, campfires, sewage and waste disposal and were effective January 1926.

By October 1925 North Bend's camp had been further improved to include a main building and six tourist cabins; eight more cabins were planned. In 1926 a fireplace was added to the main building.

Charles and Cora Hoyez were the auto park caretakers from February to September 1929. The Hoyez' were replaced by the G. A. Gurneas.

Possibly during the depression camp facilities were neglected and the mix of occupants changed. Certainly the public reputation of the auto camp declined and local children were warned by concerned parents not to venture near the area.

The auto park facilities remained in use until 1948, but by this time the S. E. McCarters were renting the area and apparently subletting the cabins. In late May 1948 all cabins and trailers were vacated in preparation for a major park renovation near the McCullough Bridge. Buildings were razed and underbrush and trees cleared. The city had budgeted $5000 to convert the area into a playground and picnic site, today's Simpson Park.

Auto Camp. Courtesy Coos Historical and Maritime Museum.

28. WELCOME SIGN

North Sherman Avenue

The increasing flow of traffic entering North Bend on the Roosevelt Highway (U. S. 101) after the Coos Bay Bridge opened, prompted the city to hang a highway-wide sign reading "Entering North Bend" to southbound traffic and "Leaving North Bend" to northbound vehicles.

The state, however, refused a permit for the sign. The city, owning the land on which the towers supporting the sign stood, proceeded. Construction began in August 1936. Because the sign might be ordered off the road by the State Highway Commission, Electrical

Second welcome sign, late 1930s. Courtesy Coos Historical and Maritime Museum.

First welcome sign. Photo from *Coos Bay Harbor*, November 12, 1936. Courtesy North Bend Public Library.

Products Co., builder of the sign, assumed all responsibility for it, and promised to defend it if any suit were brought.

City engineer, Reuben L. Cavanagh, built the concrete foundations for the 45' high steel towers at an estimated cost of $140. The steel towers and the sign were sold to the city for $790, erected and ready for use. Electrical Products Co. agreed to maintain the sign against breakage, electrical problems, paint loss, etc. for one year.

The 37 ½' wide sign, hung from steel cables between the towers, had 40' clearance from the road. Illuminated in the winter from 5 p.m. to 1 a.m., the monthly electrical cost to the city was about $14 in 1936.

In early February 1937 high winds dislodged the

new sign, twisting it and leaving exposed wires. In May Electrical Products replaced the first neon sign hanging over the Oregon Coast Highway in North Bend. (Note that the configuration of the sign, as well as the wording, differs from the current one.)

The sign, off and on over its history, has been kept fully functional in recent years. It is one of Oregon's few remaining "over the highway" neon signs.

29. NORTH BEND - GLASGOW FERRIES

Bay front, Ferry Road

The summer of 1917 L. J. Simpson donated an Old Town waterfront site (north of the Bay Park mill) to the county for a ferry connection. However with budgets tight, not until December 1920 did the county allocate

Lined up for the ferry, Glasgow side. Courtesy Coos Historical and Maritime Museum.

Ferry *Roosevelt.*

$37,000 for a vessel to be built at once. The decision was especially welcomed by farmers and ranchers north and east of the bay who thought their businesses harmed by the lack of adequate transportation.

Kruse and Banks designed and built the ferry at their North Bend shipyard. July 21, 1921, Lucile Kern, daughter of County Commissioner Henry Kern, christened her *Roosevelt* and the vessel was launched. Kruse and Banks estimated it would take another three weeks to install the steam equipment. The eighty horsepower engine and boiler were taken from the hull of a condemned vessel and brought from Multnomah County.

There were delays. By the end of September, North Bend Iron Works had finished the steam fittings and Kruse and Banks had installed her two paddle wheels. The *Roosevelt* needed only her engine and hull inspections before commissioning but these remained undone for another thirty days. Furthermore, pilings were still going in for the slips that would protect the ferry and its landings. Hopes for a full fall run disappeared.

Meanwhile, earlier in the year, Mayor Peter Loggie had the city deed the county a small strip of land through City Park for a road, called Roosevelt Road, to connect north Sherman Avenue to the ferry landing. The county's first effort to survey a road produced an unacceptable six-percent grade. In shifting their work a bit to the west, the crew cut down a number of old trees, much to locals' displeasure. The road problem was solved by starting even further west, thus, avoiding the grade entirely.

The *Roosevelt* made her first trip Saturday evening May 6, 1922. Alvy Lee, Marshfield, was captain and Charles Kime, Coquille, engineer. During the following week the ferry schedule was irregular; grading of the North Bend landing was not finished. For awhile, due to shoaling of the channel, the ferry dragged chains on her runs to stir up the silt so it could be carried off by the tide. The first year, ferry service was discontinued in late November. Heavy rains made area roads almost unusable so there was no point in operating.

When boarding the ferry locals knew to drive forward to the cabled end. Tourists, perhaps fearful of

Ferry *Roosevelt* departing Glasgow for North Bend.

driving off, had a tendency to stop in the middle and had to be directed into place. Unsecured brakes were another hazard and meant that vehicles occasionally rolled into one another.

In March 1924 the *Roosevelt* received some unexpected business. Stout Lumber Company's *Martha Buehner* (formerly the *A.M. Simpson*) struck the railroad bridge one night, knocking an eighty-foot section into the bay. Trains were blocked for four days during which the Southern Pacific used the ferry to keep passenger and mail service going.

Late in 1924 a fuss over ferry service played itself out in the local newspaper. A letter to the *Coos Bay Harbor*'s editor signed "A Taxpayer" invoked complaints in the name of farmers north of the bay. The writer griped that runs were not frequent enough and that ferry employees didn't work long enough hours to justify their pay. Beyond the complaints, the letter contained interesting information. Reportedly the *Roosevelt* was making nine trips a day, ending at Old Town. The actual crossing time was about twenty minutes.

Both County Commissioner Henry Kern and Emil Peterson made prompt replies to "A Taxpayer." They commended Captain Edwards (Herman Edwards now in charge) and his crew while reminding the public of all the extra work required of them during the rush of summer season. Regarding the schedule, the captain was given discretion to cancel a run if it was stormy or there was no business. On the matter of lying over at Old Town, "Taxpayer" was faulted for not recalling that the farmers asked for that arrangement in order to have more time in town to handle business.

On a foggy night in early November 1927 the *Roosevelt* hit guard pilings 300' out from her Glasgow landing and broke a large hole in her hull. She sank in five or six feet of water with two autos, a milk truck and five passengers aboard. Captain Thomas White was her master. The ferry was refloated and taken to Kruse and Banks for repair.

Later in November, North Bend sent a delegation to the State Highway Commission on two related local issues. First, to lobby against any change in the Roosevelt Highway, routing it east around the bay and eliminating the North Bend-Glasgow ferry, and second, requesting the state take over operation of the ferry from Coos County. In March 1928 the state agreed to assume responsibility for the ferry.

The repaired *Roosevelt*, now captained by John Graham, was no longer satisfactory. In September 1929 the larger thirty-car capacity *Oregon* was purchased in Longview, WA and brought to the bay. The *Oregon* was overhauled and her cabin shortened to increase her capacity to thirty-six cars. She went into service October 26, 1929. The *Roosevelt* was tied up, at the ready, for use when traffic required.

The *Oregon* had a six-cylinder Atlas Imperial diesel engine in her center and a screw at each end. She proved prone to break crankshafts and could be sidelined for six weeks while a new part was made in San Francisco. At such times the old *Roosevelt* took over.

Ole, in his late twenties but with a younger mental age, ran a stand at the ferry slip. He sold candy, gum, postcards, newspapers, and even smoked fish. Sometimes while talking with a customer, he would forget and leave a fish basket on the car's running board. Deck hands would spot it, sample the fish and on the return run trade the basket back to Ole for a candy bar. Some hands also took advantage of Ole's love of gambling and cheated him when flipping for candy by using two-headed or two-tailed coins.

In 1930 new ferry slips were built both at Glasgow and North Bend. The latter's was built near its original site while Glasgow's was moved a half-mile west and extended 1800' into the bay. The Glasgow move shortened the distance across the bay and also

Ferry *Oregon* landing at Glasgow. North Bend in background. Courtesy Coos Historical and Maritime Museum.

the highway connection to the ferry. By 1931 the ferry was making three trips an hour and running 7 a.m. – 11 p.m. to keep up with traffic.

Before midnight, (probably just after the ferry's last trip), Saturday October 1, 1932, three prominent Portland men bound for the bay area died when their car drove through the cable-closed north ferry approach and into the bay. The accident was discovered when the *Oregon* made her 7 a.m. Sunday run. A Gurnea Service Station wrecker recovered the Hudson sedan, with owner Paul Smith, lumber broker, at the wheel. The body of Karl Meeker, an attorney, was found opposite Empire. E. R. Joplin, an apartment house manager, was not immediately located.

Ferry *Oregon* at work. Courtesy Clair Jones.

Pressures on the ferry service continued to grow. By 1933 there was serious planning for a major bridge across Coos Bay; construction began in 1934. In May that year the *Oregon* increased her run to four times an hour. The month of July proved the busiest month ever with service for "45,094 autos, 140,432 passengers, 149 head of livestock and two double teams."

In October 1934 the state indicated its intent to give the ferry landing back to the City of North Bend. The Coos Bay (McCullough) Bridge opened to vehicle traffic in May 1936.

The *Roosevelt* was sold to Coos Bay Dredging Co. and stripped of any valuable gear. Later she was taken to a cove on Isthmus Slough and abandoned. Only her ribs remain. Reportedly, the *Oregon* was sold back to Washington State interests.

30. COOS BAY BRIDGE

Five major bridges were built along the Oregon coast during the depression. They replaced congested ferries, sped traffic and during construction provided employment for hundreds of men. In June 1933 state engineers opened a North Bend office in preparation for construction of a bridge across Coos Bay. City council granted permission for the bridge access to go through City Park.

August 29, 1933, the State Highway Commission held a public meeting in Marshfield's city hall regarding the bridge. Major C. F. Williams, U. S. District Engineer for Oregon of the Army Corps of Engineers, was in charge. Everyone interested, pro or con, was invited to express their view on a proposal for a "fixed bridge of three steel spans with concrete arch and viaduct approaches, totaling an overall length of 5,140 feet, to be constructed between Russell Point and North Bend, Oregon."

The *Coos Bay Harbor* welcomed the bridge and the August meeting noting that ship owners had been consulted, the plans were perfect and that the time was ripe. "Were it not for the president's emergency act funds for the coast bridges [this] would not have been available within the life time of most of us. Now we have the opportunity to take advantage of an outright grant or gift of 30 per cent of the total cost, and the remainder to be repaid on long time easy payments with low interest costs." (*Harbor*, August 24, 1933).

Congressman Mott, in January 1934, wired that the Works Progress Administration (after 1939 called Work Projects Administration) had approved the bridge construction. The North Bend Chamber of Commerce immediately scheduled a celebratory banquet at the Hotel North Bend. January 16, 1934, L. J. Simpson gave the main speech and Conde McCullough, bridge designer, also spoke. The men addressed a packed house - seventy-five people had to be turned away.

Low bids totaling $2,123,318 were submitted to Washington, D. C., for contracts in April 1934. Northwest Roads Co. of Portland had bid $1,529,438 for the construction of piers and approaches. Virginia Bridge and Iron Co., Roanoke, Va., bid $593,880 for the steel

Construction of Coos Bay Bridge. Courtesy Coos Historical and Maritime Museum.

spans. The span was now estimated at 5,888' in length with a 27' wide roadway and two pedestrian sidewalks. The center span's height from the water was about 150'.

The state considered imposing tolls of twenty cents for an auto and driver and five cents each additional passenger for all five Oregon Coast bridges. Busses and trucks had their own fee schedule. Everyone was pleased with the announcement that the bridges would be toll free.

Actual work on the bridge began in July 1934. In January 1935 the concrete base for a main bridge pier was poured. This was a concrete slab, eight feet thick, laid in a cofferdam 40' below the surface. The steel began to arrive at the end of March. (In July 1935 Barham Brothers, who had a contract to build a bridge over the Southern Pacific tracks at the north end of Sherman Avenue, finished their job.) In November 1935 Raymond E. Brown became the first bridge fatality. He fell headfirst to the mudflats, and died at Keizer Hospital two days later. Alva D. Smith also fell to his death six months later. He was stripping cleats from the concrete.

By March 1936 the bridge was nearing completion. Pedestrians could walk across it and contractors expected to finish well before their September deadline. Naming the bridge became an issue. North Bend citizens and groups, as well as Empire and Charleston

Design detail of a steel span on the Coos Bay Bridge.

groups, joined by the Coos-Curry Pioneer Historical Association, wanted to honor the late Captain A. M. Simpson. The Coos County Chamber of Commerce wanted "Coos Bay Bridge" and that is what the State Highway Commission selected. In 1947 the bridge was renamed for Conde B. McCullough who died in 1946.

The bridge officially opened to traffic on Saturday, May 2, 1936. Three days of area wide celebration were set aside in early June. Elongated "bridge pin" buttons were sold as a fundraiser. Myrtlewood mementos also were available. The observance was dedicated to Asa Simpson. L. J. Simpson, his eldest son, was the general chairman for the fete. Edgar Simpson, another son, brought two rail cars of oxen, wagons and stage-coaches from California for the parade. A banquet and ball also were part of the festivities. Queen Cherry Golder reigned over the event. Oregon's Governor Charles H. Martin formally dedicated the bridge. An es-

timated 20,000 people attended the celebration activities.

The *Commodore*, her four tall masts clearing the bridge deck by several feet, was the first sailing vessel under the bridge. Her passage was captured in a photo published by the *Harbor*, April 2, 1936.

Over the years, the bridge has become known locally as the "North Bend bridge." The City of North Bend's logo incorporates its likeness.

The bridge was listed on the National Register of Historic Places in 2005.

Detail of a pedestrian entrance to bridge. Courtesy Coos Historical and Maritime Museum.

31. CITY WHARF

Centered at foot of Virginia Avenue

North Bend's Street Committee closed the original city wharf, built 1904-1906, in January 1922. The choice was to repair or rebuild. When no decision was immediately forthcoming the local newspaper made its view clear. A *Coos Bay Harbor* editorial in July chastised the city for neglecting its wharf and depriving the town of steamer service. In November the editor called North Bend a seaport town without a useable wharf and suggested, as far as shippers were concerned, the city might as well be ten miles inland.

Meanwhile, in September, Kruse and Banks shipbuilders stepped forward and announced a public dock at their yard to handle freight through the McCormac steamship line. Currently all merchandise traveled to the Marshfield dock.

A $30,000 bond to finance a new wharf passed overwhelmingly in the late November 1922 election. By

City Wharf, probably after 1925 construction.

March 1923 City Engineer Reuben L. Cavanaugh had drafted plans and presented them to the council. As described, the city owned frontage from California to Washington Avenues would be bulkheaded. A "T" shaped dock would extend from the foot of Virginia. The crosspiece would be 200' long and 50' wide. This first segment began a wharf that would eventually span the city's water frontage.

It was late September 1923 before work began razing the old dock, tearing up the planking and cutting down the pilings. In December Mayor Phil Keizer reported that the city had purchased a $1500 machine to encase the new pilings in cement, a protection against toredoes (a wood boring pest). Compressed air forced cement into the pilings "firmly and quickly." Kruse and Banks provided the compressor equipment. Work began at the foot of Virginia, extended into the bay to the harbor line (the latter still being negotiated with the U. S. Government), then turned south to connect with the Stout Lumber Co. (Mill B) wharf.

The wharf extension south to Washington Avenue was built by the Cape Arago Lumber Company under an agreement with the city. The cost was $81,000. Half of the wharfage fees charged the lumber company by the city were rebated to the company to pay the building cost. The agreement specified that once construction costs were recovered the wharf would revert to city ownership.

In January 1925 an additional $23,000 bond was approved to complete the wharf and build a warehouse upon it. The new city wharf and warehouse (pilings were projected to last fifty years) was dedicated on May 10, 1925. Mayor Keizer officiated at the 2 p.m. ceremony, and after his remarks about the construction process, the Coos Bay Concert Band presented a musical program for an audience estimated at 300.

In the new wharf's first couple years there were two serious auto accidents. In November 1926 LeRoy Hise of Eugene nearly drowned when, thinking he was on his way to Marshfield, he drove his Ford off the city wharf at Virginia. He sued the city and in December 1931 was awarded $2500 in damages. November 28, 1927, Mr. and Mrs. W. J. Webb drowned when their auto also drove down Virginia and off the dock. A year later the Webb estate sued the city and asked $15,000 for the deaths. After a year the suit was settled for $3250.

June 1934 the city gave a one-year lease on its wharf and warehouse to Southwestern Oregon Equipment Company, Inc. The latter was a new group organized by locals Floyd Robb, Lorance Eickworth and William Gainotti. They aimed "to supply loggers, mills and contractors with materials for those respective lines..." Their stock was displayed in the warehouse. Additionally the company, acting on behalf of the city, had "full charge of the wharf and merchandise passing over it." They collected wharfage fees and reported monthly to the city. Furthermore, it was the firms intent to represent a steamship line(s) and re-establish regular calls at North Bend.

It is not clear that Southwestern's venture was successful. During their tenure, Jesse A. Williams, operator of the Coos Bay Crab Company, leased part of the warehouse for a crab picking plant. Williams was then part of an April 1935 deal that brought the Columbia River Packers (Astoria) to town.

The Packers Association took a five year lease on half the city warehouse and wharf. They agreed "to extend the wharf and warehouse north some forty feet making a warehouse 72 x 100 feet." The Association also planned a cold storage facility for processing salmon. No canning was to be done; the fish were shipped to Astoria. Trollers from Crescent City north to the Siuslaw River were expected to bring catches here. As part of the agreement the city was to build floating docks for the trollers at a cost not to exceed $500. Williams became the representative of the Association and oversaw the North Bend operations. In late July 1935 he shipped twenty-four tons of salmon to Astoria, the bulk from trollers arriving that week.

The new city dock and its subsequent expansions were in place for the exciting times created by the arrival of pilchards. In Spring 1936, with $7000 pledged to the city from pilchard tax receipts, plans were underway for a new wharf 300' long and 25' wide between the North Bend Iron Works at the foot of California and North Bend Fisheries property near the foot of Virginia. North Bend did the work and was reimbursed as the tax revenues came in.

In the years after 2005 federal funds will help finance reconstruction of some of North Bend's waterfront access.

City wharf. Courtesy Coos Historical and Maritime Museum.

32. PILCHARD INDUSTRY

Amidst the Great Depression transient pilchard gave North Bend and the Bay Area a brief, but significant, financial boost. The pilchard (Pacific sardine), related to herring, had been an important fisheries product for California since the early 1900s. By the 1920s processors used a technique called reduction – the fish were cooked and the meat turned into fishmeal for bait, fertilizer and animal feed. The unsaturated oil was valuable for cooking compounds, soap, linoleum and paint.

Pilchard fishing was a seasonal activity, June to October. Catches were made at night when the fish fed closer to shore. The fishing boats or purse seiners, carried ten to thirteen man crews. The word "purse" referred to the shape of the net after it closed on a catch. An average net capacity was 100 tons per catch. In the mid-1930s large schools of pilchard appeared on the Southern Oregon coast. California businessmen soon followed.

During the spring 1935 Angelo and Frank Lucido (San Carlos Canning Company, Monterey) bought the two-story warehouse (400 Virginia) from Mrs. Charles S. Winsor. The Lucidos operated as North Bend Fisher-

North Bend Fisheries at foot of Virginia Avenue.

ies Company. They opened in June with twenty employees and their first catch, just outside the Coos Bay bar, netted 180 tons of pilchard. The facility could handle 500 tons per day and had three fish oil tanks each able to hold 37,500 gallons. Each ton of fish might provide up to fifty gallons of oil. Pipes from the tanks carried the oil either to railroad tank cars or boats.

North Bend's second reduction plant, Pacific Sea Products, was owned by Knut Hovden (Hovden Food Products). He bought a 300' piece of waterfront property from Coos Bay Logging Co. and built a new plant, wharf and floating dock. Operations began the summer of 1935, but not at capacity, as construction was ongoing. The industry was considered important enough that the Southern Pacific extended rail spurs to both the plants. (Del Mar Canning Co., Monterey, built their Cypress Fisheries Plant #2 in Marshfield).

During their first July North Bend Fisheries reported processing almost 1900 tons of pilchard. They had four boats working for them but expected, at peak season, to have twice that number. Their total weekly payroll, for boats and employees, was $10,500. Pacific Sea Products, at less than capacity, reported a $600-900 weekly payroll for employees and $4000 for boats.

Purse seine fleet. Courtesy Coos Historical and Maritime Museum.

In August the industry expanded again. Two floating reduction plants arrived from San Francisco along with their fifteen seiners. Fishermans Produce operated the 480' *Lansing* and Gardenia Packing the 280' *Brookdale*. Each vessel could handle fifteen to twenty tons of pilchard per hour.

Also in August North Bend's citizens welcomed their new industry with a two-day celebration for crews and their wives. Some 1500 people enjoyed the heaping quantities of spaghetti and beef made by the fleets' cooks. Races, contests and dancing lent the multi-national gathering the flavor of Monterey's own fisherman's festival.

North Bend received its third plant in spring 1936. Carmel Canning Company, (Perry Brothers of Monterey), using the name Arago Fisheries, built a wholly piled 100' x 200' structure near the harbor line

south of the Shell Oil station on the waterfront highway.

The state taxed plant owners fifty cents per ton of pilchard brought in, ten percent of that went to the general fund and the balance to the State Game and Fish Commission. The city had to provide docks and moorage for the pilchard fleet. City Attorney John G. Mullen went to Portland in May 1936 and got from Fish and Game the promise of $7000 in pilchard receipts to build a new wharf.

As happened before, and would happen again, our region provided a valuable natural resource that was capitalized and extracted for the profit of outside interests. That said, there was considerable local benefit from these operations during otherwise lean times. People were employed, boat and other supplies were purchased and city infrastructure was improved. Kruse and Banks built Oregon's first purse seiner, the 86' *Sea*

Purse seine fleet.

Giant, for owners Robert Banks and John Graddis.

The 1937 season did not happen. The pilchard disappeared as quickly as they had come. Possible explanations were overfishing, a change in water temperature, and/or naturally occurring cycles. Vessels took only three tons in July. Boats returned to Monterey.

Hope stirred again in July 1939 when two seiners brought fifty tons of pilchard to the North Bend Fisheries. As the month wore on more boats arrived but they found no fish within a profitable distance of the bay. In early August the season was declared a flop and the South Coast's courtship by the pilchard industry was history.

Columbia River Packers Association plant with four masted sailing ship alongside.

33. NORTH BEND MUNICIPAL AIRPORT

Charles Lindbergh's 1927 solo flight New York to Paris, across the Atlantic, focused national concern on aviation. In the bay area, air enthusiasm grew and several sites for airports were under public discussion by 1929. One location was Barview where Empire Development Corporation offered 160 to 200 acres. Another, considered the Marshfield field, was the mud flat adjacent to Eastside. Yet a third was the Bangor location on the west side of Pony Inlet, north of Montana, potentially 300 acres if several properties could be acquired. The *Coos Bay Harbor* editor was clearly skeptical about a North Bend airport, noting on August 23, 1929, that "nearly everyone admits we are more in need of a city hall, athletic field, natatorium [swimming pool] and a revamped lighting system than an airport."

The Barview site never caught on. Pilots also complained about the Eastside mud flats; one, after breaking a landing wheel, declared it unsafe. So, in October 1929, with Mayor William Vaughan as chairman, a North Bend group urged clearing and grading the Pony Inlet site. J. W. Mitchell, local clothing merchant, organized a crew to fell large alder trees making an entrance to the field from north Broadway.

The *Coos Bay Times*, on October 21, 1929, reported that several army flyers, Lieutenants F. J. Williams and T. H. Barbur, were inspecting the Eastside and Pony Inlet sites. "Both were declared to have great airport potentialities." Both, however, needed signs that could be seen from the air for identification. North Bend supporters certainly worked a public relations effort for their field. City engineer Reuben L. Cavanagh announced that only $13,718 was needed to make the

Bangor field ready for planes.

In late October aviator Tex Rankin was on the bay. He performed stunts and took the city's elder statesman Peter Loggie, age 84, up for his first airplane ride. Rankin promised a report on the Eastside and North Bend sites. Additionally Lieutenant Carlton Bond, another army flyer, landed and took off from both the Eastside and North Bend fields.

"Experts for Eastside Airport Site" was the *Coos Bay Times* headline on November 7, 1929. Three of the four men above, Williams, Bond and Rankin, plus James Polhemus of Portland filed their opinions favoring the site. That the Eastside flats were already filled and centrally located were major points in that site's favor. North Bend, however, did not abandon the Pony Inlet locale.

North Bend City Council, in special session with the school board, voted to cancel all taxes due on the Pony Inlet site. L. J. Simpson chaired a delegation that went to the county to ask them to do the same. The county court agreed and instructed the district attorney to work with North Bend's city attorney to find a legal way to transfer the property for use as an airport. At a January 1930 sheriff's sale, the City of North Bend bought a 235-acre tract, the holdings of Simpson Lumber Co. and Hewitt Land Co., for an airport.

City Engineer Cavanagh earlier had suggested that it would take only $13,718 to develop the Pony Inlet site. He estimated a dike and tide box at $2100; ditch work at $1,200; drain tile $240; 1,200 feet of macadam road leading from Montana to the landing field $1800; site work $1200; and the cost of the 250 acre site $7178. The *Harbor* noted that with land donations, the property cost might be reduced to just $1600.

In February 1930 the city council authorized im-

Bennett Air Transport cabin plane. Bennett officials, from left, Elbert Parmenter Vice-President, A. A. Bennett President, Hap Roundtree Aviator. *Coos Bay Harbor* November 14, 1930. Courtesy North Bend Public Library.

provements to the airfield. Rex Brattain, of Corvallis, stationed a Waco plane at the North Bend field. The plane was used for flying lessons and emergency trips.

Brattain wanted the field improved. In March the city also bought a twenty-acre Southern Oregon Tract for airport use, paying $1600 plus taxes due. Almost immediately a contract was let for dikes and a road to the airport.

Hugh Dingman, a seven year old living at 1776 Maple, kept a close eye on the developments at the nearby dirt airstrip. Rex Brattain was the local aviation hero. One day Hugh, pulling his wagon, was bringing his family a salmon provided by a neighbor. Brattain's biplane was on the field causing Hugh to detour for inspection. Brattain asked what was in the wagon and then offered to trade a flight for the salmon. A first airplane ride was too tempting to be refused. Unhappy parents greeted Hugh when he returned home wagon empty.

The fourth of July 1930 was celebrated at the airfield. Cars were charged fifty cents to park there with the money earned going to improvements. Four planes were on hand to give rides to the public. North Bend's firemen were in charge of the celebration that included races, dances and the Browning Carnival. The *Harbor* reported "Aviation has taken hold on people, until now it is of the highest interest in any community."

The film "Sheikville Ranch," billed as "Coos County's First Complete Motion Picture" and "A Rip Snortin' Cowboy Comedy," was screened twice at the Community Building with half the gross proceeds to benefit the North Bend Airport. The late July 1930 showings included scenes from the airport, Marshfield's baseball park, Rotary banquet at the Hotel North Bend, and a fully loaded lumber schooner passing the ferry *Oregon* in the bay.

Bennett Air Transport announced in October 1930 that air service from North Bend would begin as

Air Schedule, *Coos Bay Harbor* November 28, 1930.

soon as the airfield was ready. Two large hangars were to be built at once. A one way fare to Portland of $18 was planned. An airmail contract was hoped for. A group of North Bend citizens (including Frank Muscus, Bill Reed, Joe Ryan, Henry Kern, William Vaughan, Edgar McDaniel, Dr. Russell Keizer, Robert Banks and Carl Golder) contributed $125 each to form a booster organization for the airline.

On November 1, 1930, Elbert Parmenter, vice-president of Bennett Air Transport, made a promotional flight taking seven passengers to a football game in Portland. Among the passengers were E. L. Frye, Gar Imhoff, E. J. Arms and his daughter, Janice.

Later in November Bennett Air Service began daily service to Portland where other connections could be made. The flights stopped at Cottage Grove, Springfield, Eugene and Corvallis. Ticket offices for Bennett Air Transport were at the Hotel North Bend and the Chandler Hotel. Advertisements for Bennett's Air Service disappeared from the *Harbor* in April 1931, suggesting that, with the depression underway, patronage was insufficient to maintain the schedule.

The first major air disaster for a flight out of North Bend, occurred in July 1931. Rex Brattain, owner of Brattain Air Service, and W. C. McLagan, of Mountain States Power Co., left for Springfield. While no one witnessed the accident, the Fleet plane appar-

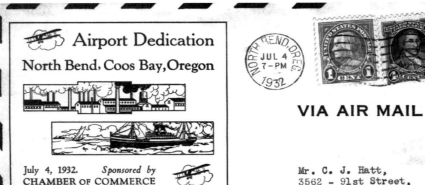

ently plunged into the ocean near the Umpqua bar where some wreckage was found. McLagan's body showed up in a week, Brattain's a month later. The latter left a wife and young daughter.

In February 1931 the Port of Coos Bay sought authority to lease, own and operate any airport. North Bend's Commissioner William Vaughan opposed such action, as did the North Bend Chamber of Commerce. But the Port Commission, in May 1931, decided to lease and operate the Eastside airport. In 1934 the Port secured some federal funding for their airport. By the late 1930s the Eastside airport, known as the Coos Bay Airport, was the more prominent "working" field.

North Bend chose to advance its own field, despite Port Commission action. The North Bend, Coos Bay, Oregon Airport was dedicated July 4, 1932. Edgar McDaniel, who as *Harbor* editor had expressed doubts in 1929, was now mayor and a supporter. The Chamber of Commerce sponsored the dedication event. A special commemorative envelope was printed. The depression, of course, kept any significant developments from occurring. Indeed, things were so quiet that hay grew on the field and the harvested bales were stored in the hangars.

In November 1935 the *Harbor* headlined "North Bend Lands Two Air Advantages." Coos Bay Air Line, Inc., scheduled commercial and passenger service from here to Portland with stops in Eugene, Albany, and Salem. The airline expected to be a feeder line for Pan-American Airways but needed an air mail contract to succeed. Additionally, a North Bend naval air base had been approved. In December news came that the federal government had approved $68,000 for construction of an air and seaplane base. Runways and a large hangar were part of the project.

Construction, begun in January 1936, was slow. In April 1937 the Works Progress Administration had about fifty-five men steadily employed on airport work. Over the summer of 1937 the W.P.A. ran an electric pump to sluice sand through pipes to fill various areas. Additionally, sand from nearby dunes was used for the field. A 400' by 1800' area was the biggest of several fills. When the fill project was done, a dredge pumped silt from Pony Inlet to cover the sand so the airport could be seeded with grass. Large bass, in quantity, also managed to come through the dredge onto the field. Only in 1939 was the dredging finished and the airfield seeded.

Airport field work. *Coos Bay Harbor* July 1, 1937 photo. Courtesy North Bend Public Library.

After Pearl Harbor, December 7, 1941, work on the municipal airport speeded. At first the two runways were graveled and oil sealed. In early 1942 a squad of seven Lockheed-Hudson Army bombers used the field. In April 1942 W. P. A. funds were disbursed to finish the airport by adding a third runway and paving all three. In May 1942, the Navy leased the airport for the duration of the war plus six months. They planned to spend over a half-million dollars on it, with no expense to the city.

On May 10, 1943, the airport was commissioned as the U. S. Naval Auxiliary Air Station, under Seattle jurisdiction. After the war, the airport was returned to the City of North Bend and run under Civil Aeronautics Administration regulatory authority.

In the 21st century, the North Bend Municipal Airport (whatever renamed) is operated through a countywide airport district.

34. SHOREACRES II

The first Shoreacres house burned the early morning of July 4, 1921. This disaster happened only two months after the death of L. J. Simpson's wife Cassie. These were tremendous losses to the founder of the City of North Bend and builder of Shoreacres. (One word was L. J. Simpson's version, Shore Acres was Cassie's preference)

August 9, 1922, L. J. Simpson married Lela Alma Gardner. They refurbished the gardener's cottage at Shoreacres adding a wing to the south. (The gardener's cottage, minus the wing, still stands.) By mid-1926 the Simpsons had adopted two girls. The difficult times of the early 1920s were easing and, as the general economy improved, Simpson's natural optimism spread from his businesses to thoughts of a new home on the site of the old. The gardener's cottage must have seemed cramped for a man used to spacious rooms.

In August 1926 word spread that Simpson had engaged Fred Magnusson, a prominent local architect, to draw plans for a 216' long by 48' wide house at Shoreacres. While some preliminary excavation began in 1926, serious construction did not begin until 1927. John Granstrom had the building contract. Working on his crew were his brothers Alvin and Sig, plus Hjalmer and Sig Anderson. Estimated cost of the construction was $60,000. The family probably was able to move in by late 1928.

The new residence had seventeen rooms, not counting entry halls or baths. The living room was a 26' x 48' space with a large stone fireplace on the south wall. Charles S. Kaiser built the fireplace, using rock brought from all over the world as ships' ballast and dumped under the docks at the "old town" North Bend mill site. The big kitchen with pantry, dining room and a breakfast room were also on the main floor's central core. A 48' seaside porch paralleled the living room. Bedrooms were upstairs.

One story wings extended north and south from the main area. The north wing had a laundry, two bedrooms for servants, and a garage. The south wing was one large room, undoubtedly intended as a ballroom, but used as a playroom by the girls. The oriental garden with its arched bridge and sculptured herons, purchased in 1915 at the Panama-Pacific Exposition in San Francisco, remained in place.

The business reversal Simpson faced in 1929, with his new Empire mill in receivership, was compounded by the stock market crash that foreshadowed the great depression. The Shoreacres home never

Second Shoreacres home, main building front entrance with north and south wings. Courtesy Coos Historical and Maritime Museum.

received finishing details or complete furnishings. The elaborate flower gardens were abandoned in favor of practical vegetable plots. Simpson's income declined dramatically. Properties all over the area were lost either to government for taxes or to those holding mortgages. Shoreacres itself was mortgaged.

In 1936 fire threatened Shoreacres. Several outbuildings, including the ranch and powerhouse, were consumed and the flames reached into the rhododendron garden. Men from the Coos Bay Labor Council helped Simpson light backfires and the Simpson home was saved.

In 1940 L. J. Simpson went through formal bankruptcy. This absolved him from all liabilities, most dating to 1930 or before. Nearly $16,600 was in secured debt, while $63,000 was unsecured. The largest portion of the latter was for improvements to the Empire mill.

Bankruptcy revealed that L. J. Simpson now owned no property, held a few shares of local, essentially worthless, stock and had his clothes to his name. The Bennett Trust controlled Shoreacres.

In late 1942, with the Simpsons' blessing, the Bennett Trust sold Shoreacres to the State of Oregon. The $30,000 price was discounted to $29,000, for cash. In 1943 the War Department leased the property and military units used the site for a radar station. The house occasionally hosted dances. At the end of the war, the property was returned to the state.

After the war the Shoreacres home stood vacant and exposed to the elements. Engineers said it would take $50,000 to restore the house. No significant preservationist movement existed. The state chose to demolish the structure, promising an observation building on its site.

Destruction of the second Shoreacres home began in December 1948. The state made good its promise of an observation building and over the years made Shore Acres State Park, and its botanical gardens, a source of pride to the area, much as Shoreacres was in its prime. Indeed, the Friends of Shore Acres' annual holiday lighting of the restored gardens continues the best Simpson tradition of showcasing the site to visitors from around the world.

Bayside view, north wing and second Shoreacres home. Courtesy Coos Historical and Maritime Museum.

SELECT BIBLIOGRAPHY

Chappell, Lyle B., "Lyle Burdette Chappell," autobiographical fifteen page typescript with four pages of "Rambling Reminiscences" appended. Chappell family.

Chappell, Lyle B., "1405 Union Avenue 1925-1975," two page typescript about the house. Chappell family.

Coos Bay Harbor, 1905-1950 (North Bend's weekly newspaper).

Coos Bay Times, (daily) selected issues.

Douthit, Nathan, *The Coos Bay Region 1890-1944*, 2nd Edition, Coos Bay: Coos County Historical Society, 2005.

Hansen, Richard, "History of the U. S. Naval Auxiliary Air Station North Bend, Oregon," North Bend: Historic Oregon Press, March 1994. Typescript copy at North Bend Public Library.

Koppy, Ann, "The Pilchard Fishing Industry," c. 2000 typescript manuscript, Coos Historical and Maritime Museum, North Bend, Oregon.

McDaniel, Deanna, "And Everybody Knew Everybody," conversations with her father, Gordon Bert McDaniel, 1986 typescript manuscript, North Bend Public Library.

Pierce, Patricia Choat, "Depression Issue Myrtlewood," North Bend, July 1976, pamphlet.

Riley, Edward W., "North Bend Airport Master Plan," October 1972. Authorized by North Bend City Council. Typescript copy at North Bend Public Library.

Snyder, J. E., "A Little City's New Community Building," *The American City Magazine*, April 1926, pp. 433-434.

Wagner, Dick, *Louie Simpson's North Bend*, North Bend: The North Bend News, 1986. (Reprinted in 2002 by Friends of Shore Acres).

Wagner, Judith and Richard, *L. J.: The Uncommon Life of Louis Jerome Simpson*, North Bend: Bygones, 2003.

Uncredited images from authors' collection.

NOTES